Gene
&Toots

Dear Henny & Chris,

Gene
&Toots

A Story of Love . . . and Recovery

*We hope you enjoy reading
our love story.*

*Love,
Marilea + Gene*

Marilea C. Rabasa
and Gene Dunne

Sidekick Press
Bellingham, Washington
United States of America

Published 2023
Printed in the United States of America
ISBN: 978-1-958808-13-9
LCCN: 2023908618

Sidekick Press
2950 Newmarket Street, Suite 101-329
Bellingham, Washington 98226
sidekickpress.com

Gene and Toots, A Love Story

Cover design by Andrea Gabriel

Contents

Part Four: SECOND ACTS

Part Five: COMING HOME

The Tale of Two Wolves

A grandfather is talking with his grandson and he tells the boy that there are two wolves inside of us always at war with each other.

One of them is a good wolf, which represents things like kindness, bravery, and love. The other is a bad wolf, which represents things like greed, hatred, and fear.

The grandson stops and thinks for a second, then he looks up at his grandfather and says, "Grandfather, which one wins?"

The grandfather quietly replies, "The one you feed."

—A Cherokee Legend

My Second Wind

From Gene to Marilea, 1/9/2001

"When I think of you, I think of Elvis' 'Love Me Tender'." Gene pulled his Gibson off its stand, strumming parts of the melody:

"On your birthday, I propose
to celebrate you in my life.
But with what words? What phrases?
What do I say?
Grateful. Happy. And wonderful.
You are absolutely wonderful.
Full of wonder, full of wonders,
voiced breathily, like you say, 'Wonderful'
at an opalescent Golden Lake sunset.

You love me like no other,
And I, you. It's been fun getting older with you.
You teach me a lot. We don't share everything,
and we don't need to.
Each of us like strangers in a strange land
(someone else said that, too)
has our own pace, our own appointments, our own children
of whom we share right pride and burning hope,
yet I never see enough of you. Just you.
Perhaps the insanities which seem to pervade our lives
like steady spring easterly breezes
are our lot, exercises which will strengthen us, balance us,

give to us a deeper appreciation of things to come,
times which we will call wonderful.
Together.

Afterthought

Then again, maybe Elvis said it better:
'Your kisses lift me higher
like the sweet soul of desire
...just a hunka hunka burnin' love...'"

"Thank you, darlin,'" I responded, glowing, as Gene returned the Gibson to its stand.

"Don't get too cocky, Toots," he winked. "I just love you, plain and simple."

"Bravely spoken, my darlin,' bravely spoken . . ." with a wink of my own.

We who can laugh well—both outwardly and at our own frailties—are doubly blessed. Just when I'd nearly forgotten how, Gene taught me to laugh all over again. Comedy and laughter are effective shelters, especially in these trying times.

As we face down COVID-19, and having received the reprieve not granted to many in the world, Gene and I want to share the love story we have lived for twenty-nine years.

We allowed ourselves to be pulled into love's emotional vortex—in midlife—bruised and battered from our own individual share of relationship wars. But there was magic igniting between us, the kind you read about but usually don't get to experience.

The last thing I needed or wanted was another man in my life. Still reeling from a divorce, my children and I were trying to survive, unscathed.

We didn't. There were wounds inflicted at that time that cannot be undone. But as surely as I must live with that, I also know that had I turned away from this second chance at happiness—

bold beginnings at a pivotal time for me—I would have missed out on a great adventure. And whatever else may be said of us by those who come after, Gene and I grabbed the bull by the horns and have ridden it for nearly thirty years.

This is the man I'd stopped hoping for. He embodied the best traits of my father, most notably his love of music and his sharp wit, with parts of my brother thrown in for good measure.

How did I get so lucky, to have found the water, the woods, the mountains, and all the outdoors—my sanctuary—in one simple man?

Part One:
WATER

"I don't need therapy; I just need my boat."
—Zaki Zaki

On the Lake

All stories have a beginning, and ours began in our childhoods, many miles apart from each other. It was in those green spaces of our lives that we enjoyed the comfort of being on water. Gene grew up in the Chesapeake Bay watershed area. My life began farther north, on a small lake, but later my family moved to a town near the Atlantic Ocean. Boats were a big part of each of our lives, a passion that ignited the chemistry between us many years later.

In 1956, I was eight years old, the youngest of three children in my family. We lived in a rural town in southeastern Massachusetts, and at the end of my street, an old iron mine had been converted into a lake. I spent many, many hours there. But inside my house was not a happy place for me.

"Can I come down and help you, Daddy?" I called to my father in the basement.

"No, I'm busy and have to get this done today. Go check on your mother," he grumbled, slurring his words.

Standing outside my mother's door, I heard the weeping on her bed. It frightened and enraged me at the same time. I didn't even try to get her attention.

Why is she crying? Maybe it's my fault. But what have I done?

Retreating downstairs to the kitchen, I dug my hand into the cookie jar and grabbed six of my mother's Toll House cookies. Wolfing them down with a cold glass of tap water, I felt no better. The walls seemed to be closing in on me and I needed to go outside. I put on my coat and went into the woods, sobbing.

My sister, a budding ballerina with many of her own friends, took little interest in me. That left my brother, Bill, ten years my senior and on his way to becoming an expert sailor. If I wanted to break out of my loneliness, it would be a good idea to take an interest in sailing. It was my brother's great love, and he would be happy to pass it on to me.

One day, Bill asked me to help him with maintenance on our first boat, a wooden Town Class our family named *Windsong*.

"Mary," he said—the name he always called me—"please run home and ask Mom for some rags. I need to get the boat painted before it starts raining. And," he called after me, "make sure they're the boat rags!"

On Lake Wampanoag, my brother taught me everything I now know about sailing. And how I loved feeling the gusts of wind blowing onto my face. If they didn't knock me over, they made me stronger.

Next, Dad bought a sixteen-foot Comet for Bill. Some summers were so sultry and hot near the lake that I was glad to have the Comet as a refuge. And it was the only quality time for us to be together. He was a good teacher, and tough. He was quite a perfectionist, but it turned me into a better sailor. Above all, he was an encouraging instructor.

"Mary, keep the sheets you're holding tight; don't let them flop around." He reached over from where he was standing to pull them in.

I should have held them tighter.

"When are we going to turn around?"

"See the buoy up ahead? We're going to go around it. Remember to switch sides when I say to."

"Okay. Do I pull in the line right away?"

What if I make a mistake?

"Let the sail fill with wind first, and then adjust your sheet. You'll be a good sailor, Mary. You're learning fast."

I love being in a boat with my brother.

A strong gust of wind startled me as I was basking in Bill's praise, but he put my fears to rest.

"Hike over more, Mary. Don't worry. Hold on to the sheet and you won't fall in."

I didn't fall in, even though we had to switch course often to reach our destination. Frequent tacking was expected in lake sailing. The surrounding land interrupted the flow of wind, which could become shifty on the water.

Tacking became an important skill in sailing, and though we often need to do that in life—switch course to get somewhere—I cheated over and over again, looking for shortcuts. Navigating my life this way was reckless, missing warning signs and important lessons.

I should have known there are no straight lines to get from one place to the other.

'Delwar' Bay

I learned to sail on the Delaware Bay off Lewes Beach, near where Dutch sailors eventually established the "first town in the first state." As a child of six or seven, I had mostly served as ballast and chief bailer, always on the leeward side of our small wooden sloop, a Barrows 18, while Mom cringed on the higher, drier windward side as the *Ghost* heeled in moderate wind. I grew comfortable on the water as a bucket-and-sponge-holding passenger, even when the sharply heeling *Ghost* almost buried the rail.

But I always wanted the tiller.

"Maybe when you're older, Geno," Pop always said.

And I recall the morning
when Pop woke me up with
"Geno, get up! Your boat is sinking!"

And sure enough
in the shallows off Lewes Beach
the *Ghost* had split along her keel
and filled with bay water.

My father also bought a Sailfish, a twelve-foot-long lateen-rigged craft with a flat surface big enough for one, maybe two. My older brothers Buddy and Chris would solo this simple, fast boat, while I sat on the sand at Lewes Beach with my sister, the oldest child, and my parents, and watched.

One such day, as Buddy beached the Sailfish, I remarked to no one in particular, "Gee, I'd like to do that."

Pop overheard me and said, "Go ahead."

So I pulled my little body up off the sand and walked over to the bow. Buddy had left her pointing into the breeze toward the water, so I had no trouble dragging the boat in.

Sailfish have one sail, a triangle of nylon set between two aluminum spars and raised from a midpoint on the topmost spar along a stubby, aluminum mast. They are friendly, uncomplicated boats, easy to sail. Once you know how.

And that was the problem. I really had no idea what I should do. Yes, I'd observed a lot, and presumably, been told a lot. I'd watched Buddy, and then Chris, sailing around the bay, going back and forth frequently. But I had done nothing myself. I had no experience handling a mainsail sheet and tiller.

Jumping at the opportunity Pop had given me, I took the Sailfish into the bay, gingerly at first, sailing with the wind and turning around easily. Heading toward an old, dilapidated, iron jetty that marked the north end of the Lewes-Rehoboth Canal, fear suddenly gripped me. As the current pushed me closer to the jetty, I found the Sailfish unresponsive to coming into the wind. So I turned the other way, letting the wind cross the back of the boat. This, I've learned, can be dangerous in a strong wind and cause the boat to capsize.

The boom snapped over my head and the force of it took me by surprise. But I controlled the boat and brought her home, tacking as much as necessary, having immense fun.

It only took that one fledgling experience with the tiller to know that I'd want to master my own boat someday.

Into the Headwind

My brother Bill only knew how to tackle the shifty winds on an enclosed lake. He, therefore, faced a quick learning curve when he participated in Marblehead race week for three consecutive summers. Marblehead was on Boston's North Shore and a popular sailing venue along the Atlantic coast. It was there that Bill learned to sail on the open sea. Winds on the ocean were generally steadier and less tricky than on lakes.

My favorite time of summer in the 1950s was during those race weeks when Bill would sail his Comet. He and Dad trailered the boat up to Marblehead Harbor, borrowed a mooring, and sailed all week.

My child's eyes didn't appreciate that critical bonding experience for them. Those eyes were jealous that I didn't have Bill all to myself. I longed to hold onto my brother as I felt him slipping away. Ten years ahead of me, he would be gone, first to boarding school, then to college, and then married, before I knew it.

Our family rented a big Victorian house set way back on a slight hill. Yet, we spent most of our time at the tony Corinthian Yacht Club across the harbor from the center of town. My aunt and uncle lived in Marblehead and moored their boat, *Allegra*, at the club.

It was two o'clock in the afternoon and all the grownups were huddling around the bar in the club's dining room, clicking glasses and appearing jubilant. My father was at the end of the bar. I nervously approached him.

"Daddy, I need to find Mom. Do you know where she is?"

"Go outside, Mary. You shouldn't be in here."

"But where's Mom? I need to ask her something."

"I have no idea where your dear mother is," he growled, turning away from me.

Smarting from his disinterest, I decided to leave. I smelled something familiar on his breath.

I went outside to watch the race. I was caught up in the excitement of waiting on the bluff to see who was coming in first, anxiously looking for my brother as the racers were returning one by one.

Bill was one of the stragglers that week, and I was terrified waiting for him to return. *Where was he? Who would help him if he got into trouble?* I was afraid he had capsized in the Atlantic Ocean. Bill and our times sailing together were all I had to hold onto. How would I be without my brother in my life?

Though I was Bill's devoted fan, these sentiments would gradually become irrelevant. He eventually grew up, married, had a family, and sent me a birthday card every January.

It had been a tenuous, short-lived alliance. After he left for school, I felt terribly abandoned. At first, he wrote a few, short letters, but then they stopped coming. I used to go into his empty bedroom, sit on his bed, and ask God to bring him back.

The sense of abandonment I felt disappeared as I grew into a woman with a family of my own. But until I met Gene, I'd been lost and unmoored without the comfort of being in a boat on the water. Gene reawakened this love in me.

We started exploring exciting new waters together, and Bill's tutelage came back to me.

Part Two:
THE BIG LEAP

"Someday you will be old enough to
start reading fairy tales again."
—C.S. Lewis

Kismet

As I straightened up my classroom after the last bell, a tall, handsome fellow walked briskly past my room, did a double take, and came back.

"Hi, are you Mrs. Rabasa?" he asked, checking the room number over the door.

"Guilty," I joked. "Are you looking for me?" *God, what a hunk.*

"I think so," he said. "I'm scheduled to sub for you tomorrow."

I had divorced my ex-husband, Angel, in 1992. We had been married for seventeen years and had three children together. A year after we'd separated, I was hard at work in the teaching career I had long hoped to continue. That year, I was a young forty-five.

"Oh, right, thank you for stopping by beforehand. Have you ever taught English as a Second Language? I should warn you about a couple of my classes." *Is this what instant chemistry feels like? It's been so many years . . . .*

After giving me a quick once-over and ignoring my offer, he started walking around and looking at the students' work on the walls.

"Are you interested in hearing about my students?" I called out to him, annoyed that he wasn't interested in my help.

Coming back to face me, he offered, "Sorry, Missus, uh, what's your first name?"

"Marilea," I responded tersely.

"Yeah, Marilea, I'm sorry. I was distracted. You've got some talented artists here," he said, sounding sincerely impressed.

"They are talented, aren't they? They're still learning English, but some can express their thoughts beautifully in pictures," I replied, taking the bait. "Do you paint as well?"

He was staring at me. Blue—*sky-blue*—eyes. Now I was the one feeling distracted.

"My mother painted watercolors," he answered. "And I've dabbled. But mostly I do photography."

Feeling his eyes on me, I looked down at the papers on my desk. "Well, do you want to see the plans for tomorrow?"

"Why don't you just leave them there? I'm late to see my mentor down the hall."

Oh, well, that settles it for me. He can't wait to get away. Just as well.

"Who's that?" I asked, pretending to be interested.

"Joan Timmons. Do you know her?"

"Sure. She's the English Chair. How did she come to be your mentor?"

"My graduate courses at Marymount. I'm trying to get into teaching."

"Yeah? I guess we're both late bloomers," I said, noting he was about my age. But I had just met the guy. Why was I looking for some common ground? "Good luck with that. And thanks for taking my classes tomorrow," I added, smiling.

"No problem. Glad to do it."

If he was late, why were his feet glued to the floor?

"Joan is four doors down," I said, leading him out of my room.

"Thanks, Marilea. I'll probably see you in the trenches here sometime." He started toward Joan's room.

"Probably. Oh, hey, what's your name?" I called out to him.

"Gene. Gene Dunne," he said, coming back to offer his hand.

Hmm. A classy, formal kind of guy . . .

"Bye, Gene. Good luck tomorrow," I offered. I barely had time to get back to my desk when he wheeled back into my room.

"What happened to your appointment?" I asked, delighted for another chance to see him and not bothering to hide it.

"Oh, she had a note on her door to come back tomorrow after I finish this class."

Well, he didn't go home. If he wanted to get away from me, why was he back in my room?

"Yeah? Well good, I can go over my notes with you," I said, glad to have more time with him.

Ignoring my comment and our reason for meeting, he asked, "Hey, do you like opera? I noticed the *Madame Butterfly* poster over there. Have you seen it? It's one of my favorites," he enthused.

"Sounds like you know more about opera than I do. But I'd like to learn more . . ."

Okay, Marilea, there's an opening if you've ever heard one. Ball's in his court . . .

I wondered what his next move would be.

"I love opera. I moonlight at the Washington Opera telemarketing. Been doing that for a year. And I sang in the chorus of *Carmen* and *Faust* once with the National Lyric Opera."

"That's impressive. My mother loved *Madame Butterfly*, which I know is one of Puccini's most well-known operas. But that's the only artist I'm familiar with. I love his romantic music." I was anxious to hold his interest.

Careful, Marilea. You're showing your hand.

"Okay, I'll call you sometime and maybe we can get some tickets. It's one of the perks of working for the Washington Opera," he said, winking.

"Great! Yes, call me some time." I tried not to sound too eager. "Here's my phone number." Jotting it down on a notepad, I felt like an idiot and berated myself.

If he were really interested, he should have asked me for my number.

Grabbing the piece of paper, he turned and started out the door. "Okay, I'll do that. Wish me luck," he called out as he was leaving.

"Yeah, good luck." We hadn't discussed the classes or my plans at all.

Oh, well, he'll wish we had.

I knew something about Gene now. I liked him. And I wanted to know more.

In-Between

Gene was a late bloomer to teaching. I had started my career in Nicaragua in 1976 when I was first married, but then I gave it up to be a stay-at-home mom. I missed my work in the classroom, and after my divorce I returned to northern Virginia to pick it up again.

When Gene graduated from college, he went to work for his father in the insurance business. But he didn't enjoy that kind of work and left the company. My father, too, had started out working in his family business and had left to pursue his own interests. An uncanny similarity. As I got to know Gene more and more, I saw how alike he and my father were.

Gene was married with two small children when he left his father's company, and he needed to support his family. He had some good friends in the plumbing and electrical trades and asked them for guidance. After studying the nuts and bolts of the business, he started working with one of them. But after about ten years of fixing toilets and electrical outlets, he was not fulfilled there, either. Gene's marriage fell apart during this period, and he was looking for a change.

In his late thirties, he decided to try to get into teaching. He had been an English major in college and loved working with people. So he took some teaching courses at Marymount

University, George Mason University, and the University of Virginia in order to get certified to teach in Virginia. That's about the time when I met him in my classroom. He was easing himself into the profession by substitute teaching, the same path I had taken before I was hired full-time.

Gene loved teaching English in Arlington County where I, too, was working. He stayed with it for more than a dozen years, and he also taught General Educational Development (GED) in the evenings. I believe that the two of us working in the same field was a bolster to Gene. He saw me never miss a day of work, year after year, and he felt inspired. All the after-school meetings and professional development helped us both nurture our gifts. Hours of grading papers described much of our lives together. And in short time, when I decided to attend graduate school and had to curtail being with Gene to write long papers, he was further inspired. This was one of the ways, early on, that Gene knew I was good for him. I brought out and encouraged his talents in the classroom. It was a potent factor in his attraction to me.

He is also a connoisseur of Shakespeare plays and loved teaching them to students. Oh yes, Gene knew Shakespeare and loved to share what he knew. An actor at heart, he tried performing some of the plays with his students. Once, he was teaching *Richard III* to a bunch of yawning boys:

"Mr. Dunne, why should we read something about people who've been dead for five hundred years?"

"Danny," he said, as he continued his performance. He couldn't resist moving as though he were on a stage, feigning villainy in King Richard's face. "Does this look dead to you? Do you know any bad people in the world today who will do anything for ambition? That's why we still read Shakespeare: because what he wrote about is relevant today!"

Just as I did for nearly twenty years, Gene easily came alive in the classroom.

Old Rag

Oh God, it hurts. I'm still wearing this heavy cast and mad at myself for getting drunk on a Sunday afternoon two months ago.

At forty-six, I had never broken a bone in my body. Not once.

But now I was using alcohol and overeating as a crutch to deal with life's disappointments and frustrations. And I was breaking bones.

I had met Gene just as I was hitting the reset button in my life. He breezed into my classroom to substitute for me with all that charm and those good looks and I was swept away. I know I fell in love with him first, and I began pursuing him, taking him to see Puccini's *Turandot* at George Mason University. In the pouring rain. But—not even a kiss goodnight.

Afterward, he stayed away from me. He'd been wary: a recent relationship had ended badly and he was being cautious.

I reacted to his distance one day by drinking too much brandy, an increasingly frequent pastime. The day after an ice storm, I sashayed outside to shovel my icy driveway and fell down before I even got started. Tickets to see one of my favorite childhood plays, *The Little Match Girl*, were in the car, and I drove into the city to see it anyway. With high boots on, I didn't realize what I had done to myself. I experienced considerable aching and pain, so I elevated my leg during the performance. But I couldn't wait to get home and look at the damage.

Once I got back—barely able to remove my boots—I saw the swelling and suspected I must have broken my ankle. A trip to Urgent Care and an X-ray confirmed my diagnosis, and the nursing assistant wrapped a cast around my right leg, foot-to-knee.

Gene took over my classes for a few days while I was home getting used to my cast. He left this playful note on my desk:

"You have an inviting classroom, Toots. I'll sub for you anytime. Boing!"

Hmm, not even a kiss goodnight last month, and now all of a sudden I'm Mae West.

The following month, around my birthday in January, Gene and I surrendered to our physical attraction. He took me to a performance of *The Dream of Valentino* at the Washington Opera. Sitting up in the nosebleed seats, we couldn't keep our hands off each other, brazenly necking during the whole second half, my cast notwithstanding. That's how it began, in January 1994, and now he was taking me hiking up Old Rag Mountain on the edge of the Shenandoah National Park.

"Gene, I'm still wearing a cast. Can't we wait until it comes off?"

"No. It's a beautiful, sunny day and I really want you to see the views from the top."

"The top? You're kidding. How am I supposed to hike in a cast with only one good leg?"

"Marilea, look at it this way: you've still got another good leg."

This kind of banter would characterize much of our relationship in the ensuing years: me, fearful and projecting the worst; Gene ignoring obvious difficulties and focusing on silver linings, injecting humor into many situations. This is precisely why, despite some bad times, Gene is good for me and I can never bear to be away from him for long.

I'd been given a second chance in midlife to be with a gorgeous hunk of a man who was my long-forgotten fantasy—not because of the handsomeness or intelligence or love of boats and music, all of which were considerable. My fantasy was so much simpler than that, so much more elemental. I dared to dream that I might have the chance to hike or go boating or start over with a good man, who did nothing more than fall in love with me at a time when my family didn't need that complication.

We faced a formidable headwind, but behaved as though the wind were at our backs. Formidable and risky—but irresistible.

"It's as if a childhood dream were a possibility now," I wrote in my journal in 1994.

Shenandoah

One trip we took into the mountains included Henry, Gene's best friend from high school. Henry had just met his present wife, Pam, and Gene was anxious for us to meet. As members of the Potomac Appalachian Trail Club, we rented a cabin, complete with a woodstove, and reveled in winter hiking for a few days along the spine of the Shenandoah.

My ankle had healed since the early December spill on my icy driveway. To protect my ankle now that it was out of a cast, Gene bought me a first-rate pair of Merrell winter hiking boots. I was a novice, especially at practical things like wearing the best clothing for winter hiking. Gene taught me about many things: the value of wool socks, how they keep you warm even if wet because they dry from the inside out, and the danger of cotton if it gets wet because it dries from the outside in—while you're shivering and possibly suffering from hypothermia. It looked like the four of us were going to be enjoying the outdoors a lot together, and I needed to be properly outfitted. I gradually gave away much of my cotton clothing and replaced it with polypropylene and other breathable clothing.

"Hey, babe, how many layers are you putting on?" he said, observing me dressing in the morning. "You need at least two

At the cabin.

with your skinny butt, maybe three in this cold," he added, his eyes fixed below my waist. It warmed me that Gene was so protective of me.

"Not right now, babe. Henry and Pam will be back soon from their walk to make breakfast. Let's get a fire going in the woodstove and warm the place up."

His eyes met mine and I saw disappointment. I kissed him softly on the mouth, squeezed his hand, and turned back to the pile of clothing I was putting on.

"I think our friends would love to come back to a toasty cabin while we have breakfast together," I suggested.

"I'll go chop some wood," he agreed.

My introduction to Henry had been comically awkward. He and Pam had just arrived, and I was in my upper bunk in the cabin peeing into our chamber pot. I finished up without dribbling, and lazily looked up, just as our friends walked through the door.

Gene threw a towel my way to cover up, and I welcomed them with a kittenish grin: "Hi, you two. Welcome to our cozy cabin, outhouse, and kitchen—all in one! Nice to meet you!"

The Teacher

As a child, I spent a great deal of time outdoors. My parents sent me to camps that would nourish my love of nature. Camp Treasure Island in New Hampshire was where I first set foot in a canoe. The following year, they sent me to Camp Mary Wellman in Topsfield, Massachusetts, closer to home, where I slept in my first tent. Two sailing camps in Cape Cod—Camp Wono and Camp Quanset—continued my brother's tutelage in sailing. These camps indulged my love of nature in every way they could, and all those experiences would prepare me for my partnership with Gene thirty-five years later.

The spring of 1994 brought with it lots of rain—a prescient occurrence if ever there was one—as we started planning our first canoe trip to Canada. Second only to Gene's great love of sailing was his knowledge of canoes. He had enjoyed several paddling trips in recent years with Henry. The most recent one in La Tuque, Quebec, might have killed them both in a car accident.

He and Henry had been on their way north in Quebec to paddle the Mistassibi River when they crashed off the main road north of Trois Rivières, and the low-lying ravine they plummeted into provided a soft landing pad. They both spent the night in a local hospital, but neither of them was seriously injured.

Gene had a T-shirt made—"Disaster at La Tuque"—lest anyone forget what a survivor he is. He enjoyed plying me with his canoe trip stories, playing them up big as he convinced me to take up canoeing with him. There was still that river to conquer.

Standing on my front lawn at my house in McLean, Virginia, Gene asked, "Have you ever been in a canoe?"

"Years ago," I responded, "at Camp Treasure Island in Lake Winnipesaukee."

"Remember anything?" he prodded.

"Like what?"

"Steering strokes."

"No . . ."

"J-stroke?"

"No . . ."

"So, you were in flat water. What do you remember?"

"I sat up front and pushed my paddle around in the water. I had no idea what I was doing. The camp counselor who was steering from the stern started giggling, and the next thing I knew we were both in the water, about ten feet from shore, knee-deep and laughing hysterically."

We sat down in silence for a while. Gene thought about the scene I had described. Harpo and Chico, Curly and Moe, and Laurel and Hardy with paddles. No, none of that would work, not in serious white water.

"How old were you?"

"I don't know. Maybe eight."

"And you never got back in a canoe in all these years?"

"No, I haven't. But I'd like to go again."

"Okay. Let's go look at boats."

That weekend, Gene picked out a Mad River Revelation, a sturdy, Royalex canoe, and REI became our new best friend. A week later, my tutorial began.

"Let's start with the paddle," Gene said. "It serves a variety of purposes. You must get comfortable with it and learn how to control the boat equally well from starboard and port, bow, stern, and amidships."

We stood on my front lawn, four paddles on the grass beside the brand-new Mad River Revelation. I smiled. He frowned.

"Really, the best way to learn is to do it. On the water."

I looked at him in silence. "And when do you propose to do this?" I challenged.

"Now," he answered. "Pick up the boat by that grab loop of nylon line running through the bow." He pointed forward and moved to the rear. "On three, just lift her up to your knees. Ready? One, two, three," he counted, and lifted the stern two feet off the ground. The bow stayed put.

"Oof!" I sputtered. "I can't move this thing!"

"It's easier to handle in water," he counseled, and walked back to where MAD RIVER CANOE stood out in bright script in the middle of the boat. Gene leaned over the canoe amidships, grasped each gunwale, and in one smooth motion, rotated her over his head.

I blinked. "Holy shit. What's that thing weigh?"

"About eighty-five pounds the way I've rigged her," he said from under the boat. "And she's a canoe, not a thing. Feminine—not neuter. Feminine—but tough. A canoe, a whitewater canoe, tandem, rigged out with a center seat for solo paddling, knee-padding, bow and stern flotation, skid plates bow and stern, hull treated for UV, rails sanded and rubbed down. Only the best for you, Toots."

He walked the boat over to his Ford Ranger, our chariot that in subsequent years would take us all over the United States. New Yakima racks sat close to his cab roof. Gene easily slipped the canoe over the restraint ells that steadied the boat on top of the truck, secured the hull, and tied the ends securely.

"C'mon. Let's go."

"Where?"

"Let's go up to Violette's Lock and put the boat in there. We can practice in the canal. You have a lot to learn about bow pad-

Paddling on the Thornton River.

dling. It's critical, because your ability to read water will be my best defense in avoiding disaster."

"What disaster?" I asked, naïve and alarmed.

"Babe, if we're heading downstream in class-three rapids and crash into a rock, even in a Roy-alex canoe, we could wipe out pretty badly. Any serious damage to the canoe would cripple us. And up in the hinterlands of Canada, we might find ourselves stranded. No, reading water is a basic skill all paddlers need to master, especially in white water."

"Okay, I believe you. I'll be a good student." Then, brightening up, I added, "Hey, it'll be an adventure!"

Baptism in Big Water

Three months later, we went on our first canoe trip to Canada. Having failed to get up to the Mistassibi River the year before, Henry and Gene, persistent as ever, determined to go back and try again, this time with two novice women paddlers. What were they thinking? That we would bring them good luck this time?

It's a good thing Gene and I were so in love, because on many levels the trip was an unrelenting nightmare. For one thing, I missed my kids more and more over the two weeks we were gone, though I knew they were safe with my colleague, John, who had moved into our house.

The first actual trip challenge was driving through La Tuque and inhaling the paper mills without gagging. It was a horrid, cloying odor that permeated the air everywhere we went. I imagined the residents didn't even notice it anymore. And Gene and Henry had already had enough bad memories of that town.

Weeks of incessant rain meant the water was very high. It was so high that some of the places where we had hoped to camp had no beaches. At our first stop on a lake, we put in the canoes at the high-water mark and dragged them and all our camping gear right onto the outlying brush. There was no flat spot for our tent, and we didn't care; we were exhausted from paddling all day. We just wanted to collapse somewhere and be free of bugs.

"Don't forget the ground cloth first or we'll get soaking wet," Gene hollered as he scrounged around for dinner food.

"Not likely, Gene, we've pitched the tents on top of a cluster of blueberry bushes. Wish we could levitate a foot off the ground instead of smashing the bushes to death," I said with a groan.

My mouth was watering just thinking about the blueberry pancakes that Pam wouldn't be able to make in the morning. This was just the beginning of our trip.

The black flies swarmed so voraciously that I risked total dehydration by covering up in all my waterproof gear. It was like living in a permanent sauna. Gene and the other couple would apparently rather breathe and get covered with bites than suffocate like I was. I even put a net over my head, eating and smoking through a hole I'd fashioned.

Pam and I spent much of the evening before bedtime squashing the flies on the ceiling of each other's tents. This variety of black fly didn't resemble large flies or mosquitoes. No noise to warn us, just attachment wherever they could sense blood running under the skin, and then suck away. Real vampires. Even as covered up as I was, they managed to find plenty of exposed skin, and I was miserable, itching for most of the trip.

"They need to eat too," Gene reminded me, as if that would soften my attitude toward the little parasites. It didn't.

Relentless rain continued. We packed up the next day, hoping to find a better campsite on another island. But we spent hours inside—which is bad when you're camping in a tent and would like for one evening to sit outside and just enjoy the evening air and night sky.

"Where are you going?" Gene asked, annoyed that I was leaving him alone in the soggy tent.

"If I don't get some fresh air, I'm going to scream," I barked, forgetting that late in the afternoon was usually showtime for the big female mosquitoes. Not the black flies. They were always around, latching onto exposed skin and the veins just under the surface, always hungry.

I was so claustrophobic from huddling down inside a saturated tent that I didn't care anymore about the rain. I just donned my rain gear all the time, except when I was in my sleeping bag, and covered myself with a tarp. This was serious, relationship-threatening stress. Our evenings weren't romantic at all. But at least Pam and Gene were excellent cooks. We ate well, starting with lamb chops that first evening on top of the newly squashed blueberry bushes.

The rain had even more serious consequences during the day. It was dangerous to paddle many of the rapids. When Gene warned me to have a lot of respect for hydraulic power, I didn't know what he was talking about. Soon enough, though, I would learn firsthand what he was referring to as I felt the swift and powerful current propelling us downstream. He put me in the bow of our Mad River Canoe because I didn't have enough strength to push a loaded, eighty-five-pound boat from the stern with two people in it.

I wanted so much to please him. He was a taskmaster and he pushed me hard, just like my brother used to. So in that sense, his actions were familiar and comforting.

The black flies were persistent and nonstop day and night, never giving us a moment's peace, and even covered up, I grew crazed with itching. We were all exhausted. The water was so high that we had to portage all around the rapids—carry all our camping gear and our canoes on our backs—to get to a safer place to put our canoes in the water.

I had seen the movie *Deliverance* many times, and I learned how dangerous boating in big rapids could be. Gene and Henry knew this too, and they took no chances with their girlfriends. It was necessary to portage through the woods in order to arrive at safer water levels before proceeding downstream.

"Okay, this is a good place to take out. There's room here for Henry and Pam to pull up behind us," Gene determined, knowing full well how much work faced us of a different sort.

I groaned for the umpteenth time but did my part. I was a willing student and in love. I took orders well.

First, I hopped out and tried to balance the boat so that Gene could unload it, piece by piece. Our friends performed the same operation in their boat, and we had a number of water packs dotting the shoreline and two canoes waiting to be carried through the bug-filled woods to a safer spot to run the rapids.

Slogging through the woods to our destination, Pam and I took turns with the water packs on our backs. Free hands were wasteful, so we carried our paddles as we walked, careful to keep our balance. The guys took turns with each boat over their heads. Royalex canoes are heavy and challenging to carry.

I fell behind with Pam and we got a little lost, relying on our whistles to find the men. Disorganized, anxious, tired, and sick of bugs in the woods, we made our way back down to the river and were relieved to be back in moving water continuing downstream.

When we did dare to run a rapid out of sheer exhaustion, my place in the bow was critical to alerting Gene about the rocks ahead. This is where Gene's teaching me how to read water would become paramount: how to tell from a crashing wave if a rock was up ahead. I was extremely nervous, and concentrated hard to remember what he was telling me about which stroke to make.

"Marilea!" he yelled as we rocked the boat in and out of the high rapids, "keep your eyes peeled for crashing waves ahead." I was straining to hear him as his voice competed with the rapidly moving river. "When you see one, I need you to steer us away from it with your draw and cross-draw strokes. We're moving too fast. I can't maneuver us to safety by myself!"

"I'm trying, Gene. I'm doing my best, believe me. I'll be the first to feel the impact if we do hit a rock," I countered, feeling the pressure building.

I heard the urgency in his voice, but I was trying to hide mine. I wanted so much to impress him, but I felt like a dummy and way out of my element. To me, it had started out as an adventure with my sexy new boyfriend. To Gene this excursion was maybe not life and death, but we were facing the real possibility of an overturned canoe on our first outing. He wanted to give me an unforgettable experience. He also hoped to seduce me into being his canoe partner. A disaster on the Mistassibi, with little hope of a timely rescue, might have put an awkward damper on our new-found passion.

We managed to avoid crashing against any rocks, thanks to my good eyes and timely recall of the basic bow strokes I'd learned. But what a catastrophe it might have been otherwise. Luckily, we were in our sturdy Royalex canoe, but I still would have felt re-sponsible if we'd hit a rock at the speed we were going. These were Class Three/Four rapids, standing waves at shoulder level, and I must have been out of my mind to agree to go on this trip with him.

But, deeply in love, I would have gone just about anywhere with Gene.

Masks

In 1948, the year I was born, it was generally accepted that a fat baby was a healthy baby. Even before my body changed at age twelve, I had been a compulsive overeater. Back in the 1950s, we didn't know what that was; I was just a child whose hand was always in her mother's big red cookie jar. That led to obesity in college and a lot of fat-shaming.

"Marilea," my mother harped, "what are we going to do with these hips?" She grabbed my haunches from behind until I felt her fingernails.

"I don't know, Mom." I twisted away. "I'll go on another diet. My friends at school know a surefire way to lose weight." I hoped to please her.

That new diet involved eating all the food I wanted and making myself gag afterwards, just like the Romans used to do. Bulimia was epidemic in my college dorm; I had a lot of company. It was not a new diet or even a remotely healthy way to eat. It was just another shortcut. I wanted to have my cake and eat it too—literally—without gaining any weight.

This led in the 1960s and 1970s to another shortcut: diet pills. I needed to do something to stop eating all the time, and amphetamines took my appetite away. For nearly a decade, I used those pills to eat less and to elevate my mood. I loved them.

But soon afterward, I got married and stopped using drugs. I knew I wanted to have children, and my drug use would pose a threat to them. This was an inflection point in my character development, a place where I chose health over self-destruction. Unfortunately, though, my demons never completely went away. I slid back into compulsive overeating, though I never used amphetamines again.

Then, as I watched my marriage to Angel end, I took up drinking as well. My eating disorder lessened and faded in subsequent years, but I was simply replacing one substance with another.

Alcohol. I was dangerously close to becoming my father.

Mr. Dad

I have many fond memories of the early years with my two children, Patrick and Bridget. My drinking was heavy, but I managed to shag flies with Pat and take them both roller-skating regularly. We went hiking on Old Rag Mountain and all over the Hawksbill area, sometimes camping overnight. I took them to church, and to baseball games in Baltimore. Pat was in a youth basketball league, and I enjoyed coaching him and his team. In her teens, Bridget and I worked three fall weekends at the Renaissance Festival, dressing up and enjoying ourselves as much as the paying customers did. Both kids were with me at the premiere of *Star Wars* on a beautiful afternoon. The local news was covering the opening at the Uptown Theater where I made an appearance, telling the newsman, "I'd rather be golfing."

Gene had been divorced since 1986, and his children lived with their mother close by in Arlington. I met Bridget soon after her father and I met in my classroom. He took us to a matinee of Donizetti's *Anna Bolena* at the Kennedy Center. Was Gene suspecting that our relationship might become serious? When he and Bridget performed together at annual summer Renaissance festivals, I tagged along, happy to play second fiddle. This was their special time together.

After the Mistassibi trip, life went on with my three teenagers and me. Angel and I had been divorced for two years and—angry about the divorce—he did not share custody of the children with me. He was preparing to remarry and to move to Rome for three years where he had accepted a stellar posting as the deputy chief of mission to the Vatican. He was generous, however, with financial support, and that enabled us to keep the house in McLean, Virginia, where I'd been living with the kids. I was it, raising our children on my own.

I was also an alcoholic and a compulsive overeater. Adept at wearing masks, I could be secretive, even with Gene. At that point, early in our relationship, I was too ashamed of my eating disorder to open up to him completely. When I indulged in this compulsion, I was always alone.

On any given (bad) day, racing home after school I might have an hour to myself before the kids got home. *An hour to myself* . . . to raid the freezer for ice cream and gorge on it with the cheap pastries I'd picked up at 7-Eleven—always followed by two cups of any hot liquid to loosen it up in my stomach so that it would come up easily. In the toilet.

Ah, relief. From what? What was I getting rid of in the toilet? My evil juju?

I wasn't. And it would keep plaguing me, this self-flagellation, until I did some serious work on myself and challenged the part of me—that brokenness—that insisted I was a bad person and didn't deserve to be happy.

Unresolved guilt had led me to a therapist's chair a few times: once while I was still living in Greece, and then later, in McLean, soon after we all returned to the States. But apparently I wasn't ready to dig down deep and do the work, and I left therapy soon after I met Gene.

This was the dark, self-destructive side of my character. Self-loathing still competed with any self-worth I'd managed to muster—and had for most of my life. It was always a battle between the "two wolves" in me. Not until I was much older, for example, could I gracefully accept a compliment.

"Babe," Gene used to say, "Try to take what I say to heart. You're a fine skater now; it's all come back to you. Don't put yourself down!"

Overeating and purging were so wasteful and unhealthy that I felt it would repel anyone close to me. *If Gene only knew the real me, how I deserve this wretched feeling of guilt I'm heaping on myself, he would be gone in a heartbeat.* How little I trusted my ability to be loved at that point, certain that the "real" me would push people away. There were two of me: the attractive, fun-loving teacher that Gene fell in love with, and the self-destructive bulimic who feared being unmasked.

A year after the Mistassibi trip, two since we'd met, Gene and I decided to try living together. My house was big, even with my three children, and we were tired of running back and forth to be together. So he put many of his belongings in storage and brought what he could to my house.

Also, Angel's absence would leave a big void in the children's lives.

"Angel," I had almost pleaded before he left, "can't you extend your tour in the States, at least until Carter graduates?"

"This is the dream job I've been waiting for since I joined the Foreign Service, Marilea. I will not give it up," he asserted without apology. "And the kids can visit me at Christmas. I'll take them skiing in the mountains there. They'll love it."

Riddled with guilt, I felt unworthy of asking Angel to make another sacrifice. Our separation had already cost him a great deal: the life he had dreamed of with me and his children was over.

So, Gene moved in during the fall of 1995. He would never try to replace my children's father, but he did feel it would be helpful for us to have a man around the house.

Annie was sixteen the year Gene came to live with us, and she was showing signs of rebellion. Though many teenagers do, I see now that it was the continuation of events that began when I divorced her father. Another family tragedy would come to light as our family members attempted to grapple in different ways with the changes in her.

One night, Annie came home at around two o'clock in the morning, well beyond curfew. I'd been wringing my hands all evening worrying, and Gene confronted her when she was about to enter her room.

"Annie, what is the meaning of this? Your mother and I have been frantic wondering why you didn't come home and imagined you were injured or something else terrible had happened. Where have you been?"

"Oh, fuck off, asshole. You're not my father, so leave me alone!" She slammed her bedroom door in his face and went to bed.

Feeling inadequate, helpless, and terribly concerned, Gene joined me in bed. We slept fitfully that night. Annie had set her boundaries clearly: *Don't try to replace my Dad. I'll do as I please, and don't interfere!*

But my daughter knew she'd gone too far. She tried to make it up to him soon afterwards by asking to go canoeing with us on the Potomac River. Gene was thrilled that she'd reached out to him, and though she never went out with us again, we had a pleasant afternoon boating with her at Violette's Lock where Gene had instructed me the year before.

Annie was impossible to read. She went out of her way to appear normal, functional, and even successful on the surface. She always earned good grades in college, worked diligently at one part-time job after another, never had a car accident, and never missed an appointment with her therapist. Her overture to Gene was another attempt to cover up her dark side.

I seemed to be Annie's role model. She may have sensed that I, too, had secrets. She hid her dark side from all of her family, just like her mom. We knew there was something simmering beneath the surface, but in spite of numerous attempts to break through her isolation, I was unable to get inside her head.

Caroline was also plenty rebellious, often refusing to go to school. Sitting by her bed on far too many mornings, I pleaded with her.

"Please go to school, honey. I can't keep calling in sick for you."

"Mom, I really have a stomachache. I just need to rest in bed."

She knew the clock was ticking, and I had to get to work. I didn't have time right then to enter into this debate.

"Okay, Caroline, I'll be home right after work to see how you're doing. Please call the school if you need me."

Enabling my daughter to avoid responsibilities was bad for both of us. I felt guilty, and she floundered. I did get her into therapy when she threatened to drop out of school, and it helped her get back on track. She graduated but refused to walk with her class. Six months later, I watched her drive away to California in her Mazda with her best friend. This was her way of dealing with our dysfunctional family: putting three thousand miles between us. It was hard for me to let her go, but I thought it was the right thing to do.

Carter kept to himself: to his studies and to his job. He went paintballing, though, with his best friend. A shooting sport was aggressive by definition. And, years earlier, when he was still in elementary school, I'd given him a punching bag to express his feelings. There was plenty of anger under the surface as he listened to his parents arguing. All the children grew up in this dysfunctional atmosphere and suffered through it—one of the reasons I was determined to remove them from a battle they couldn't win.

We kept on with our busy schedules, all five of us putting one foot in front of the other, trying to keep all the plates spinning. But there was little interaction between Gene and my kids. And while I was finishing two years of graduate school courses to get certified in English as a Second Language, I was just as neglectful of Gene's kids as I was of my own. We both could have made more of an effort to bring our children together and do things with them. It's as though we walled ourselves off from the rest of our family to avoid conflict. Gene and I sometimes lived in a world apart from everyone else.

But that world would soon come crashing down.

Having failed to build a happy family the first time around, Gene and I remained equally resourceless about creating a functioning, blended family. That would require much work, and I was already overwhelmed. Between Angel leaving the country, nurturing my relationship with Gene, attending to the demands of my teaching job and graduate school, and wrestling with my demons, it's a wonder I had any energy to be emotionally present for my children. On top of all this, I lacked many parenting skills. I was simply too attached to my own agenda.

"Mom, can we go to the store? I need some stuff," fourteen-year-old Caroline implored.

"Not right now, Caroline. I need to take a nap. I'll take you in an hour," I lied.

I'd been resting on my bed and I'd heard Gene hurriedly approaching the bedroom. My heart started racing as I saw the door open. It was like a scene from a movie.

According to some experts, the height of a woman's sexuality is in her forties, and that was true for me. Gene was a delicious lover and had lots of experience. Still young enough to experience the "itch in my pants," I was appreciative of Gene's sensuality. It had always been a happy way for us to connect.

Gene's time living with us was nevertheless short-lived. As content as the two of us were to be together in the same house, resentments were becoming apparent: Gene and I were too wrapped up in each other, distracting us from our five teenagers.

And it wasn't always honey and full moons.

Eighteen months earlier, when Gene and I were planning that first trip to Canada, I had concerns.

"Honey," I fretted, "I don't feel right about leaving the kids for two weeks. It's too much time away."

"They'll be fine with John, Marilea. Don't we deserve an annual vacation ourselves?" he replied.

"They're not your kids," I countered, feeling resentful—and anxious.

My head told me from the beginning that Gene and I were moving too fast. But my heart told me otherwise, and I allowed myself to be swept away. My anxiety about our relationship was hovering in the shadows. I should have been laser-focused on helping my children get through the divorce. Instead, I was rushing into another romance.

Timing is everything in life, and this was not a good time for us to be starting a serious relationship. I felt that we needed to live separately so that Gene would be freer to pay attention to his new teaching job and we could give the kids more of our attention. God knows they needed more of it from me—especially Annie. Their father—about to be remarried—would soon be living in Rome. They must have been feeling abandoned.

Gene and I both felt sick about separating. Yet although we'd been impulsive at first, it was gratifying to learn that we could step back long enough to see what we were doing. And then—instead of ignoring the mistake and plowing ahead—that we could follow through with the separation and find out what that would mean to us.

"Gene, this isn't working for us right now. Perhaps we've acted too quickly, hoping the kids would accept you and me as a couple so soon after my divorce," I told him. It was hard for me to confront Gene with this hard reality.

"Okay. You're right," he said. "I'll get my own place. But I'm not happy about this. And I'm not sure that my leaving will improve things for you at home."

"Maybe not. But I have to try to get closer to my kids. With Angel leaving, I'm all they've got."

He found a house in Arlington near the new job he would be starting in September and he moved out. Gene and I stopped seeing each other for several months. It felt like I wasn't going to get a second chance at love after all, and my world felt bereft of the excitement I had enjoyed with Gene. For the time being anyway, our romance was over.

We did stay connected, though, sending flowery poetry and letters back and forth. Separated as we were, it soon became apparent that we didn't want to let go of each other.

"As silken streams descending from the clouds
that shroud the distant hidden peak above,
her golden falling tresses tumble, rough as love,
yet supple, round her glowing face. Hair crowds

around her shoulders soft, alluring, warm
and pressed against my naked chest; her eyes
and mine meet deep and peaceful as she lies
beside me with her head beneath my arm.

A smile but briefly flits across her lips
and with a sigh she rolls to me again
and kisses wet and urgent strain my brain.
as down my torso slow she slips those lips . . .

I wake and find myself alone and miss
my true, real woman's loving, perfect kiss."

—Gene to Marilea, October 1996

"Maybe I don't know any more about love than the poets. I just know that my body and mind warm like a fire when I'm in a room with you, or when I'm feeling your firm and powerful direction from the bow of our canoe. It's difficult to imagine my life without you in it. I can only plod along like the rest of us and love you as best I can for as long as I can and not worry about how you are loving me. That's vanity at work, not love, and it's love that keeps me moving toward you. My fears would be better spent cultivating my own garden of flowers and enjoying them.

So take these words I write you as another in an ongoing series of communications from me to you. I'm a better writer than talker, I think. I invest this time in writing to you because I love you and I want us to go on together. There have been a few men in my life, but it is you, Gene, who has inspired me to open my heart again to love. In spite of everything, my world is a richer place because you've been in it. Be well, my darlin'. I miss you."

—Marilea to Gene during their separation, winter 1997

Sneaking Around in Indiana

"Hey, Henry, would you be up for a canoe trip this summer in Quetico? I know you've been wanting to paddle around those unspoiled lakes," Gene asked his friend over the phone.

"What? Just the two of us?"

"No, let's bring the girls. We'll have more fun, and we'll need their help."

"I thought you and Marilea had broken up. What happened?"

"Nope. Can't live without her, it seems. She helps me get things done; she might even be good for me. What can I tell you? I really love her!"

"Oh, wow, congratulations. I'm happy for you!" Gene could almost see Henry beaming through the telephone.

By spring 1997, Gene and I were determined to give our relationship another try. We continued living separately, doing our best to keep the focus on our children and our teaching jobs. But we rendezvoused often at his place after school, spending hours and nights together like a couple of love-sick teenagers making up for lost time.

To celebrate, we decided to meet Henry and Pam that summer in Ely, Minnesota. We would hire Piragis Northwoods outfitters to fly our boats and us into the lakes on the Canadian side. Henry knew the man who ran trips for the company; he would become a valuable contact on subsequent trips there.

Our friends flew to Ely and rented a canoe. But Gene and I had added to our fleet a forty-five-pound Kevlar Malecite for flat-water paddling. We drove our newer canoe from Virginia to Minnesota on top of my little Corolla sedan. On the way back, atop my teeny sedan, we were also hauling another canoe to Pennsylvania as a courtesy to Piragis. The trip west was cramped enough.

Pennsylvania seemed endless on the Interstate. The wind shear from the boat slowed us down considerably. Torture. I couldn't wait to reach Ohio, and then I felt more of the same. It wasn't until we got into northern Indiana and I could smell moisture from the wind blowing across Lake Michigan that I felt the relief of water.

The relief of water. As adults, neither Gene nor I ever got used to being separated from the boats and salt air that defined so much of our early lives. God, how we missed it.

Entering Indiana Dunes State Park, we fell back into our childhoods for a little while. Sand dunes! This wasn't Nauset Beach on Cape Cod. These were dunes caused by the wind blowing across Lake Michigan, one of the largest freshwater lakes in the world. The dunes were tall and white, and it surprised and comforted me to see them so far away from the east coast. But no salt air . . .

When we'd had our fill of dunes and fresh water, we headed back south to the Interstate. On the way, we'd hoped to camp in our tent to save money. Further down the road from all those beautiful white dunes, we drove into an RV campground around eleven at night. A foul odor woke me from napping in the car, but it wasn't a skunk. Skunks have a distinctive smell all their own.

"Let's get out of here early, babe," Gene said, turning to me and wrinkling his nose. We had the whole place to decide where to sleep since there was only one car there. He decided on a small site at the end of the campground.

"Maybe we can find a better place down the road to rest. But don't forget to leave the fee in the drop box," he instructed as he pounded in the tent pegs.

"What a boy scout," I muttered under my breath, in no mood to be generous.

We were "sneaking" because I had no intention of paying the fee. The campground was dirty and unkempt, with litter everywhere, unemptied trash cans, and a dreadful stench in the pit toilets. I felt like it was unsafe to stay there. And from the looks of it, others agreed with me.

We definitely picked the wrong place to drop in overnight, and I left no fee at the campground before we left.

But ten bucks? Parks don't run themselves. How could I be so cheap?

Argo

After we all arrived in Ely, a Piragis pilot flew us into Argo Lake on his de Havilland. Landing there on a beautiful, cloudless day, the first thing I noticed was the silence. Maybe there was a duck quacking or the buzzing of bees. But other than the wildlife, there were no sounds of human activity.

On Argo Lake, 1997.

Henry and Gene preferred Quetico Provincial Park, because a limited number of boats were allowed onto the lakes every day. It was quiet. And no motorboats. *Heaven.*

When it got too hot, we would often paddle in the buff, and that summer it was unusually warm. The area was actually experiencing drought conditions, so fires would be a serious hazard, and there had been several fires in the area recently. But since we were in the land of 11,842 lakes, we never thought seriously about fire hazards!

The lake water was a deep brown from the tannin in the thick carpet of evergreen needles. At first I was put off by it, certain that the water was dirty. But no: just brown from the tannin. And swarming with life.

"Gene, what are those black things on your legs? You're bleeding!"

"Marilea, they're just leeches. I don't even feel them. Get me a stick so I can brush them off."

I had them too. When I swam in Lake Wampanoag years ago, I believed that the bloodsuckers on my legs were sucking the evil out of me. That bratty child still popped up in my behavior now and then. *Maybe I should have left them on for a bit longer . . .*

We hopped from lake to lake in our canoes, portaging short distances only when necessary. Camping opportunities were delightful on these lakes in Quetico. They were dotted with an abundance of little islands. We could pick and choose a different one every night. No overused campsites filled with people, trash, campers with noisy generators, and barking dogs. There was practically no one else there. One of my favorite campsites/islands had several blueberry bushes full of juicy, ripe blueberries, this time free of our tents! In the morning, Pam made the most delicious blueberry pancakes I'd ever eaten. Henry had hauled real maple syrup!

Flat-water paddling was nothing like white-water canoeing. The rush in high rapids, as they had been on the Mistassibi River, was intoxicating. If we were lucky, the water would look like glass on these lakes. But if there were a strong headwind, we'd have to work much harder to get anywhere.

The Ojibwa Indians had lived up in those parts for hundreds of years and we marveled at the pictographs they painted onto the rocks. Their descendants would continue to live and work up there.

Many of them were firefighters, and that would one day be important to us.

Fire!

Quetico was simply enchanting, so much so that all four of us went back two years later for an encore. And it was quite a show.

This time, Gene and I flew to Ely, Minnesota. Piragis again flew us and our rented canoes into Argo Lake in Quetico Provincial Park. As soon as we landed and got all our gear together, we decided to separate and do some paddling on our own. Sometimes, Gene and I just wanted to be by ourselves. But as a foursome, we worked well together, sharing tasks and meals. We agreed to meet before dinner at a pair of islands that had been recommended to us. The islands themselves lay about three hundred meters from the heavily wooded forests of the Canadian Shield mainland.

"See you at the island," I said. Henry had a map and compass in hand. Bright sunny day, big cumulous clouds parading across the blue Ontario summer midday warmth. I figured he and Pam would set a point-of-compass route across open water to the marked campsite a guide had marked out for us at Piragis, where we had picked up our boats.

We had done these trips before—a week or two out in boots and backpacks, or in whitewater canoes, or lakers, and many shorter trips between just Henry and me. All four of us smoked.

Camel regulars, the original walk-a-mile-fors, the man's cigarette.

Henry and Pam unpacked lunch and announced they wanted to scout Black Island before paddling over to the unnamed rocks about five klicks distant as the crow flies from where they stood and we sat. I'd been correct. They would paddle by compass over open water to a large, uninhabited island—they were all uninhabited, except for the faraway, every-other-day sighting of another canoe party—and instead of making a beeline to our campsite, they would bump an angle into their navigation and cover the trip in two long, straight legs. I hugged the shore. Exploring Argo at a leisurely pace kept Marilea and me forever hugging the irregular shoreline, really the best way to see where land and water met. This was where so much of the flora and fauna were visible.

I hadn't traveled fifteen hundred miles again to feel bound to adhere to straight pathways in Quetico Park. There was a time and a place for hard, fast paddling on Canadian lakes—watch for squall lines dropping quick from big, puffy, smiling clouds—but dawdling into coves and gliding silent through shoreline shadows pulled me strong toward wooded hills along the quiet lake waters. I paddled like a Native American, somewhat aimlessly, hugging the shoreline. Compass bearings were, after all, at best mission-relevant, and everywhere magnetically variable on this planet, and certainly subordinate to the peace I would find guiding a canoe over quiet, dark waters a ways away from the city. I liked to hear the dip and drip of paddle and the slip and slide of, yes, plastic over lake wind wavelets. Ah, silence! Peace! The warm tranquility of passing the lazy August day paddling, serenely exploring deep woods.

I went there for the quiet. I went there for the beauty. I perceived best in the quiet. I went there for the grace of paddling the quiet waters through a decent block of time away from my daily routine.

I had developed a deep appreciation for the quiet of Quetico, which was, of course, not really quiet at all. There was the wind, the wind over the water and through the trees, and the intermittent buzzing of insects, friend and foe, rising and falling in the air; an occasional splash of fish rising; and the paddle slicing the water and the boat coursing along with its cargo.

Marilea and I had a lovely, leisurely paddle in the general direction of our campsite. The weather was clear, hot, and dry. Very dry. Tinder dry.

Our water that day was smooth, with only minor ripples to reflect the bright sun of our warm summer day. We saw a little of the lake, but we had been on the water since 8:00 a.m., and the long summer twilight was best enjoyed with camp set up early, by five, say, tent pitched, kitchen set up, savoring a slow dinner when you were hungry, but zipped up in the tent when dark fell about ten. Just after dark, the mosquitoes emerged. Depending on where you were, they could come out much sooner. It was best to be inside.

We circled the higher of the two small islands on the map, and found a smallish put-in at the bottom of a somewhat steep, rocky climb. Up twenty meters, we found a relatively flat campsite, a lovely spot, and made camp. We started water to boil for our dinner on a very flat, cleared cooking spot, away from the dry accumulated deadfall of the forest. We were careful about cooking. And smoking. I always took a canteen of water for dousing and drenched my crushed-out smokes. Made it a ritual.

We had a nice spot picked out for our friends, but Henry and Pam decided to camp on the flatter island two hundred meters from us across an azure shallows. They paddled over, though, to share a pleasant dinner. After dinner, Marilea took our canoe out solo for the first time and paddled around our little domain. While I cleaned up from dinner and walked the island, she enjoyed a quiet Canadian paddle.

Night fell. From inside the tent, Marilea and I listened for half an hour as thousands of whining thumps, sounding like a drum roll, convened on the stretched nylon, cocooning us from the flying hordes outside. We talked a little, made love to the nightly aural onslaught, somewhat carefully, respectful of and thankful for the thin, strong walls around us.

We got up early the next day. I did most of the cooking, and we had hauled a lot of fruit—apples, oranges, and dried bananas— so Marilea and I enjoyed a big breakfast.

Getting up from our cook site, I ascended the rise. Henry and Pam were up too. It looked like she was doing some baking, as well. A plume of smoke arose from well behind their tent. I absently wondered why she'd set her cookfire so early. And so far from their tent.

Marilea and I cleaned up our kitchen, secured our campsite, and packed some munchies and water into a daypack. We humped down the rocky slope to our boat, launched it, and paddled over to the other island.

We made it there in quick order. I wanted to walk the other island. Each island in Quetico was a little different from the next, and close neighboring islands are not so common.

So I said my good mornings and accepted the offered coffee and fresh bread, but set the coffee down to cool awhile, and taking the bread, excused myself for a quick walk. I walked down a semblance of trail, heading toward the cookfire, and munched down the warm, tasty bread, eyes down to where I stepped next as I worked my way into the woods. Stopping short with the last of the bread in my mouth, I looked into the forest.

It was on fire.

A low, orange carpet of flames, burning deadfall, was dancing across the forest floor and filled my vision. Flames were climbing low branches and tree trunks everywhere I looked.

I turned and ran the way I'd come.

"Hey, Henry! Pam! Pack up! Your island's on fire!"

I yelled the same message two or three times as I ran, and everyone at their campsite was busy crash-packing their gear when I got back moments later. We tossed everything into the two canoes, loose, and skedaddled.

As we were paddling, a rising, growing column of thick black-and-gray smoke and the oncoming flames outlined the thick shoreline vegetation. The burn was close to the water but inland yet, and working its way toward the lake.

And higher. Into the canopy. While we sat offshore, the fire was growing. If the upper levels of the magnificent island spruces flared and the fire somehow jumped to the mainland, a fairly impressive conflagration could ensue.

The four of us enthusiastically chose to return and put up some resistance until, hopefully, help arrived. We landed at the campsite, left the canoes on the beach, and took deep breaths as we approached the fire.

We had little to fight the fire with in terms of equipment. We used our paddles, our hands, bailing buckets, and a hastily devised plan of attack to limit the damage one of us had apparently caused.

There had been no lightning. Spontaneous combustion was highly speculative. Somebody set a spark off . . . but we would be much too busy for the next three hours to dwell on such trivial matters.

Marking off a defensible area, a line in the forest around the burn, Pam and Marilea worked with paddles and water to halt encroaching hot spots, mostly by sweeping debris clear with their wooden paddles. Henry and I worked on unlit snags, hauling mini fuel depots clear of the fire. We lifted, levered, dragged, and bullied a lot of lumber out of immediate danger, and cleared a swath of pine needles between what was lost to fire and what we had hoped to save. If only the cavalry would come . . .

We were careful. Pam got a little far in with a half-gallon of water, trying to douse a baby fir, and the flare-up singed her hand and arm. Henry and I got closer up to the edge to try to break up flares and spreading, orange puddles gobbling up the thick layers of dead, dry detritus. We used the plastic paddles to push the pine apart, burning pine needles away from those yet to ignite, and had to snuff out fires on the blades of them now and again.

It was tiring work. And hot. I brought some water bottles and we all drank a lot of water. I tried to resist the urge to remove my shirt. Back to work.

We fought as hard as we could. And as long as we could.

Maybe three hours into the fight, I knew, and Henry knew, that we were losing it. We had contained the fire horizontally. But the flames were climbing the trees.

We could do nothing about that.

And although we had cleared something of a dead zone across the forest floor, the area already burning when we had started our fight was getting hotter. The pockets of flame just out of our control joined up, linked up, grew up, and attacked small trees in the forest in front of us. Low branches of bigger trees, too, and the flame-speckled floor of the woods oozed outward like orange lava and burned like a fiery carpet rolling magically my way.

I stopped to rest a moment, took a swallow of water, and folded my arms across my upright paddle. My eyes fell on a lovely maple a few meters to my front, in the territory I knew was lost. It was perhaps ten meters tall, thriving and full branching, packed with leaves and standing, young and defiant, full of beauty, full of grace, and in the fire's path.

It torched. Like a struck matchhead, the entire tree was engulfed in a fireball.

Time to leave.

Hurriedly, we paddled off the island into the narrows between the other islands and watched the fire spread. We consoled ourselves with the effort we had made—a good one—to stop the fire. But we were pretty glum.

Pam answered the unspoken question.

"I think I did it. Morning shit in the woods. Tossed the Camel. Didn't think. God, I'm sorry."

"Pam, Pam, come on," Marilea insisted, offering her a hug and a shoulder to cry on. "It could easily have been me. I smoke too. Please don't blame yourself. It was an accident."

A few moments passed in silence. Then we heard the 'copter.

They landed after a five-minute hover over the burn. The helicopter perched down on the flat rocks around Henry and Pam's campsite.

We paddled over to the high island and off-loaded our friends' gear, helped them pitch camp, made up some lunch. We talked.

By the time we had gobbled down our food, we could see four guys left by the helicopter as they went about their task. They tossed two large pumps into the lake and fired up a fairly quiet compressor and soaked the flat island for the next twenty-six hours. Occasionally, an axe and chainsaw duet would end with a large, barely smoking tall tree dropping from sight, and sometimes one pump would sprinkle and the other pulse. Often a pair of them would fish, and they would sleep in shifts since the pumps ran all night.

We went over when we figured we wouldn't be in the way and we introduced ourselves.

George, the crew chief, and Stanley, the assistant crew chief, were two men with thick Ontario accents. Stanley said little, but we talked with George a while.

They caught no fish. They were finishing up a meal from lunch pails—sandwiches, chips, sodas—when we paddled up to talk to them.

George confirmed the previous night's absence of lightning and voiced some doubt as to the likeliness of spontaneous combustion. Pam fessed up, and George said to her, "Well, don't feel too bad. It was an accident. You shouldn't burden yourself with this. We got it under control. I'm sure you will remember this for a long time."

Turning to the rest of us, he said, "And youse showed a lot of courage and intelligence in going back to fight the fire. Youse made our job a little easier. We might have lost the island if youse had just left. Or the fire might have spread to the mainland. Youse did well."

We passed a few moments in idle chatter. George introduced the pump man and the chainsaw man, firefighters Terrence and Harold, both full-blooded Ojibway from the reservation. I asked George, one of two White chiefs sent to the fire with two Native Americans, why the 'copter had hovered over the fire a while before landing.

"We wanted to make sure we could land there and I wanted to call off the bomber."

We let that sink in. Evidently, a flight crew had at least begun to scramble in order to dump an airplane tanker load on the fire.

A nagging question emerged.

Would we be charged for this affair?

We had essentially confessed, and I envisioned a large fine. George seemed to sense our discomfort. He immediately set our minds at ease.

"Not gonna charge youse. It was an accident. Youse stayed and helped fight the fire. Thank youse for that. As to the cause, like I said, accidents happen. Up here, we have arson."

"You mean people set these woods on fire on purpose?"

"Yeah, can youse believe that?"

The helicopter picked them up a few hours later, and we loaded up and moved on to another island the next morning. The four of us couldn't bear to remain there and witness the damage we had done, smoke still rising from the burning embers.

Loonies

It would take some time to move on from thoughts of the fire, but we were in the middle of a spectacularly unspoiled lake in southern Canada and determined to appreciate all the quiet and beauty still around us.

One day on Argo Lake, we passed a most spectacular sight. We were far enough away from the feathered wonders not to frighten them.

We were a kilometer, maybe two, away from the islands where we were camping. The late afternoon sun blazed in the western sky, but despite the glare, we both picked up motion on the open water ahead. And a slight wind shift—correcting to the ever-present headwind we had avoided by paddling along the shore—brought a cacophony of honks and whistles and trills supported by a tympanic flapping and splashing, all growing suddenly in volume as Gene and I went quiet, paddling like interlopers to eavesdrop on the noise. He reached for his camera.

Loons they were, twenty-five at least, or thirty, maybe more, carrying on in a way I had heard about on the Nature channel, doing what I'd call a mating dance, a mad, accelerating, flap-splash-dash of webfoot and feathered wing. One, then three, and now four would start up, all calling their hearts out for ten or twelve seconds before settling easily back down into the water to serenely turn and paddle back toward the center of attention: one, perhaps more than one, sedate bird maintaining a respectable distance between our boat and her floating parade. The squalling was continuous. The whole entourage paddled a little ahead and off to our right. When one bird landed back on the lake, two more took off.

Did the winner call his heart out more than the others? Was he squalling louder? Was he more persistent? The frenzied circle of feathered males gradually faded from the female's vision. One by one, the male loons flew away, leaving the female with her chosen mate. She saw only him.

As soon as we returned to Virginia, Gene painted a picture of the loon dance ritual. The "Loon Dance" is hanging on the wall in our kitchen, a very tangible memory of an unforgettable trip.

Gene and I had only been lovers for a few years by then. But what a simmering tutorial it was for me. Our time together had become a breathtaking return to my teenage years, when sex and being in love had been completely new to me. By the time I was middle-aged, I never expected to relive the wonder of first love I'd experienced as a much younger woman. Something stirred in me whenever Gene and I were in the same room. For just a moment, other people and details faded into the background; I saw only him. And I felt something come alive, an energy that I hadn't felt for a very long time. With Gene, although I knew otherwise, it seemed as though everything were happening for the first time.

Fires are often set deliberately to encourage new forest growth.

The forest we set to blazing has regenerated beautifully.

The sun is down now but,
Opeongo's waters, iced,
gleam white under the risen full moon.

No Johnson two-stroke outboard
to scream through the silence,
and the loons are gone.
but wildlife unimpressed,
witness the night,
and forage as they have for untold nights,
keeping the stillness
with watchful tread.

—Gene at Quetico, 1999

Part Three:
BACKGROUND NOISE

"Life goes on."

On the Homefront

In 2000, Gene and I were busy with our jobs, together, but still living separately. Angel had returned a few years earlier from his posting in Rome and he needed to sell the big house where I'd been living with our children. They were either living away or in college, and we saw no reason to keep it. We sold it in a delicious bidding war, and with my share of the profit, I bought a small condominium. For the first time, I owned something by myself, and I relished the feeling of independence it gave me.

"Hey, Mrs. Rabasa, which way do you want the bricks to go?" George was my faithful gardener, following me to my new place, but with no zoysia grass to mow through. He was a brick mason by trade, so I was having him redo my patio and add some attractive flower beds.

"Just use the same pattern you used at the other house, George. I'm sure it will look great. And please pick up some bushes and colorful perennials at the nursery. I want to enjoy the view of my little garden."

My little garden. I had something of my own now. Something I had earned and could afford to keep. I was not dependent on

Angel or any other man to support me. I felt as though I could stand on my own.

Gene was a frequent visitor, of course, since he lived right up the road from me. But he did not enjoy sitting on my compact patio, barely able to accommodate a table and a few chairs. He felt cramped and confined, no doubt dreaming of living in bigger, more wide-open spaces.

I quit smoking cigarettes around this time, ending a twenty-five-year habit. It was the right thing to do, and for a surprisingly good reason. My daughter, Annie, had been developing a serious problem with substance use disorder. Our family had been crippled by too much of that, in myself, most of all. Seeing Annie so vulnerable to the temptations around her, I wanted to model something healthy for a change: show her that quitting nicotine could be done.

Nicotine was one substance I could successfully give up, although overeating and purging still plagued me at times. At this point in my life, the drinking was not excessive, but it would become so later on as I kept blaming myself for Annie's illness. Substance abuse in some form had always been my "solution" to cope with life and my own lingering demons.

I cheated, over and over again, looking for shortcuts. Navigating my life this way was reckless—missing warning signs and important lessons.

All five of the children lived through the divorce of their parents, and none of them got through those periods unhurt. They were emerging as young adults, but still in need of their parents' assistance.

As much as we loved each other, we loved our children more, and tried to help them when we could. Caroline had relocated to San Francisco, and I put her through college while she worked part-time. Carter had graduated from the College of William & Mary, lived in D.C., and loved his work in the tech industry. Bridget would graduate from Virginia Commonwealth University where she studied acting and the performing arts. Patrick was struggling, and while Pat was in college and working on a degree in filmmaking, Gene entered into therapy with him for several years. He had always tried to help his son in any way he could.

But it was Annie, my middle child, who was our most heartbreaking casualty.

The fire that burned part of that little island in Argo Lake reflected what was coming to light in my own life. Gene would witness me trying to put out another fire, one much, much closer to home.

Annie had been hijacked by a devastating disease, and it was stealing my daughter away from herself. We couldn't help but be swept up in the tumultuous sea of change in my beautiful daughter. She was morphing into a drug-addled stranger.

A new anxiety was building up in me and I developed insomnia. My doctor prescribed a mild sedative, Ambien, to help me get to sleep at night, but it wasn't always effective as I tossed and turned in bed. If Gene was with me, he didn't get enough rest, either. We were both red-eyed and fatigued on many mornings, but we went to work anyway. My work ethic rubbed off on my partner.

Somehow, Annie managed to graduate from George Mason University in 2004, in spite of the methamphetamine and cocaine abuse. She crashed on the sofa in my basement, on and off, oblivious to my attempts to help and support her. She was perilously hooked on those two drugs.

"Annalise, what is this white stuff in a bowl on the dryer?" I asked, suspecting the worst, and furious.

"Oh, fuck off, Mom. And don't you ever dare to touch my stuff again!" she responded with fire in her eyes.

That's right, offense is the best defense.

Was I just a nuisance to Annie, or was I now the villain in her eyes? I told her to sleep elsewhere and then started going to recovery meetings for families of substance users. But it was difficult for me to grasp most of the concepts in the program. I was, at that point in my life, incapable of admitting that I was powerless over Annie's disease. Facing that reality was counterintuitive for me. It seemed like I'd be abandoning any attempts to save my own child. After all, had I not been a poor model for her with my own deceptions regarding substance use disorder? With so much self-blame, how could I decide I was powerless now to help her?

There was much for me to learn about substance use disorder: how to properly treat it; how to survive it.

And in trying to survive one of a parent's worst nightmares, my gratitude to Gene for dedicating every day to helping me get through it . . . what can I say?

Boy, what a nice guy.

Gene and Peg

My mother liked Gene from the beginning. She could see how much we had in common, and she genuinely delighted in my pursuing a relationship with him.

From 1994 until our retirement in 2008, it was a rare summer that Gene and I, teachers with the same vacation time, didn't visit one of the wondrous national parks in the United States.

But after the school year ended, and before we went anywhere, we most often went to see my mother Peg in Massachusetts. We were glad to spend some quality time with her. By 2001, she was ninety-one years old.

For a traditional special dinner with us, she always had Gene go to the lobster pound for some fresh crustaceans, just as Dad used to do every Friday night in the summer. We lingered over our work to get every piece of lobster meat, while Gene did most of the talking. Mom was fascinated to hear about our canoeing adventures in the Northern Woods of Canada, and Gene was a great storyteller. Angel had been instrumental in showing me many parts of the world while we were traveling in the diplomatic service. But I had known little of my own country. Gene not only knew many of the most alluring national parks, he was determined to share the wealth of his experiences.

"Peg, you wouldn't believe your daughter. It had been raining on the Mistassibi River every day for weeks. It was still raining while we were there and the water was very big."

Wide-eyed and curious, Mother asked, "How can water be big, Gene?"

"That just means that there was a lot of water in the river, the rapids were very high, maybe a class three or four, and pretty dangerous to negotiate."

"Why were you in dangerous rapids?" she asked with alarm, looking from me to Gene.

"Well, that's the thrill of it, Peg. If canoeing is too easy, it gets boring."

"I really dislike flat-water paddling, Mom," I piped in. "White water is much more fun and less work."

"What do you mean?"

"In flat water, Ma, I have to move the canoe forward with my paddle. That takes work, and if I'm in a headwind it's a lot of work. But whitewater is the turbulence—sort of like underwater foam—created by gravity and speed pulling the water downhill over rocks. We just use our paddles to maneuver around the rocks."

"Rocks? That sounds scary! What if you hit a rock?"

"Don't ask," I said, remembering how terrified I was as we had eddied out more than once to avoid a big drop. "Gene's a good teacher, and we usually avoid trouble."

"I'd rather be safe and bored," she ventured, concerned about our recklessness.

"Well, that's you, Ma." I didn't want to sound patronizing, and signaled Gene with my eyes to move the story into "safer waters."

"Most of the time the water was so big, Peg, that we portaged. Do you know French? Portage means to carry everything: our canoe and our waterproof packs on the paths along the river."

"That makes better sense, don't you think?"

"Yes, up to a point. But what's the point of a canoe trip if you're just dragging all your gear through the woods? Our canoe weighs eighty-five pounds. And I gotta tell you," he continued, ignoring the alarm in my eyes, warning him not to go where I saw him going, "on the last day, your daughter and I were so tired from portaging that we ran the rapid—and it was thrilling. We're still here, aren't we?"

Seeing Mom's discomfort at our risk-taking, I grabbed Gene by the arm.

"Okay, time to clean up all the lobster mess. Why don't you take a shower, honey? We have an early start tomorrow."

Taking the hint, Gene got up from the table, approached my mother from behind, squeezed her shoulders affectionately, and poured on the charm.

"Peg, you don't know your girl at all."

Flattered by his warmth and attention, but a little baffled by what he meant, she responded, "Maybe not, Gene, but I'm glad you have so much fun together." She appeared mollified.

Just like my father, once upon a time, in the early days of my parents' courtship, Gene had the ability to sweep my mother off her feet and she thanked him for it. I know he reminded her of my dad, who had died in 1985. She absolutely glowed around Gene. I believe she saw my father in him as a much younger man, before alcoholism had changed him so much from the man she had married. Every summer that we visited her, we enjoyed another lobster dinner, even though she didn't like lobster. And, I am sure, she welcomed another visit from "the ghost."

Though their marriage had been difficult, Mother wished she had understood more about the disease that ended my father's life prematurely. By the time he was seventy-four, his body had been ravaged by smoking and alcoholism. He died of a massive heart attack. Now that she found herself alone, time had softened my mother's attitude about him. She had many regrets.

"I miss your father sometimes, Marilea, and I wish I'd been kinder to him," she confessed while Gene was in the shower.

"Mom, I'm certain he knows that. You did the best you could with what you knew. And I know you'll see him again."

"Do you really believe that?" *Always the skeptic . . .*

"Absolutely, Mom. We'll all be together someday."

Did I choose my father the second time around? There's no question that I saw my father in Gene, who had been an unrecovered alcoholic all of his adult life, until 1986, seven years before I'd met him. But even before I knew about my lover's alcoholism, I was drawn to him. He had an irresistible charm and a sense of humor that recalled the father I had longed for as a child.

Dad had rarely paid attention to me, but with Gene I finally got him—and the best of him at that. If Dad had stopped drinking and found recovery as Gene did, I might have had a chance to know him better.

My partner of nearly three decades still goes to meetings nearly every day. We're often crossing each other on the road, Gene going to his recovery meetings and me going to mine. Putting his faith and trust in a power outside of himself—whether it's God, a plant, or a group of people—is a discipline that has led him into the peaceful waters of recovery for many years. Gene prays every morning, a valuable exercise that keeps him grounded in his faith and free of the obsession to drink alcohol.

I never masked my drinking around Gene in the same way I did my purging. Perhaps I felt less shame about my drinking, because I knew he was a recovering alcoholic himself.

During Gene's seven years of sobriety and recovery meetings before we started dating in 1993, he had learned that no one could have made him stop drinking until he was ready to face and wrestle with his own demons. He wasn't about to ask me to face mine. He knew from experience that it wouldn't work.

Sometimes I am asked why I didn't interfere with Marilea's drinking. The answer is simple. I learned years ago that telling an alcoholic what he or she should do would be counterproductive. Telling a lush to slow down or quit would usually be politely ignored at best, or the source of unending strife at worst. My not drinking taught her by showing, not telling, and had a better chance of success.

Or maybe I just had my hands full staying off whiskey myself. I love Marilea completely, but I'm not her keeper.

Today, we are committed to our twelve-step recovery work, and we support each other unconditionally. Gene is my best friend. He has always been my biggest cheerleader.

And sometimes he lets me beat him at Scrabble.

Trespassing

Gene has a special fondness for some of the national parks in the East where he and Henry, as college graduates, had backpacked along the Appalachian Mountain Trail. They enjoyed more than one trip to the Smokies in North Carolina and Tennessee. Upstate New York, in particular, held many vivid memories for Gene.

We went camping there in 2002 near Gene's old college haunt, Hobart. We discovered once again what often happens when people stumble into spaces meant for other creatures. We step on insects, swat black flies and mosquitoes, and curse all of the rodents going after our food—the harmless little chipmunks and squirrels, to name a couple. But larger animals require much more outfoxing and tact. Bear barrels, for example, are sturdy containers with a special bear-proof lock. A bear barrel can hold a number of items and fit into a backpack. We always rent one in bear country, and eventually, we bought our own.

Bears are almost mythic nowadays, especially grizzlies. They're still around out West and in Canada and Alaska, but far fewer in number; we keep destroying their habitat. While camping on Mount Marcy in Adirondack Park—though we didn't actually see the bear—we knew he'd been there.

What was really scary was that Gene and I were sleeping in an open lean-to. If the bear had really been starving, he could have attacked us. As it was, he settled for going after our food.

Gene, like all responsible campers in bear country, suspended our provisions on a line out of the bear's reach, including the locked, bear-proof barrel. We went to sleep in the open air, confident that our food was safe.

As usual, I woke up early while Gene snoozed and went to get our food bag so that I could make coffee. After a long day of hiking the day before, I was hungry for a nice, salty breakfast. I could taste the succulent bacon and eggs already, and was glad I'd remembered the salt-and-pepper packets we always snitched from Burger King.

Sprinting back to the lean-to, I woke up Gene. "Honey," I whispered to him, "the line is down and the pack is strewn all over the ground. Did we get beared?"

"No, I put it up plenty high enough. There's no way he could have reached it," he asserted, opening his eyes.

"Then how did it happen? No camper would do that to another camper."

"There's always a first time," he suggested. "Is there any usable food left on the ground? Did the egg holder protect the eggs? Any sign of the bear barrel?"

"No. I'm gonna follow the food trail and see where it goes."

"Okay. But if it leads to another tent, come back here before you say anything to them."

Especially out in the wild, Gene has always been fiercely protective of me. He knew I lacked his level of experience in camping outdoors. I was blissfully ignorant of basic survival skills, including ways to troubleshoot a catastrophe. Gene also knew how campers, by weathering their own discomforts, could become testy and territorial when confronted.

But he needn't have worried. The trail led straight down a hill to a deep stream below. I scanned the area for signs of food, and there, plopped in the middle of the stream, wedged between some boulders, was the bear barrel.

I waded out to the boulders, up to my thighs in cold, running water. Grabbing the barrel and slogging back to the bank, I decided to see what I could salvage, and then turned around and made my way back up the hill to our campsite. All I found were torn wrappers stripped off our energy bars, shredded baggies, the Oscar Meyer wrapper, and some unwashed cutlery, minus the food.

"Honey," I said to Gene as he was packing up in the lean-to, "it makes me very nervous that a full-grown bear was this close to us while we were sleeping. If he was hungry enough to steal from our pack, what might he have done to us?"

Turning to me, he tried to allay my fears. "I guess you could say that our food saved us. The bear found it and left us alone. But some people feel we would have been safer in a tent, rather than a lean-to. What they don't realize is that bears don't attack people without a good reason. And we're invisible in a tent. Lesson learned."

In a rare moment of chagrin, Gene gave me a big hug as we both felt relieved to have lost only our food. For a wilderness camper, food is life. We're visitors in the bears' backyard. We keep forgetting that they were here first and have every right to forage for our food.

Losing most of our food was a disaster for us, so we had to pack out early.

Turning in our rented barrel at the park entrance, we got a knowing smile out of the ranger. The claw mark of our visitor was clearly indented on top of it.

"Better luck next time!" he said with a laugh.

Into the Woods

Back in the 1950s, alcoholism was more whispered about than openly discussed in my family. My father was an alcoholic. I was the youngest child, and by the time I unexpectedly arrived, the elephant in the room that we'd all avoided had grown bigger. I frequently listened to my mother crying on her bed. There was great stress in the house. Both my brother and sister married early, and I remained at home with little chance of escape. Too often, I felt clamped in a vise between my warring parents.

When I needed relief from the tension in the house, I went outside to my home in the woods. That was my safe place. It was designed around a huge, granite boulder. There were four bedrooms and a family room, which served as the kitchen as well. Sometimes I used old sheets with a window cut out, and there was an old radio someone had left by the brook that I put on the kitchen table, a turned-over crate.

With a vivid, child's imagination, I invented fantasies that lifted me up, at least for a while. They were never a waste of time. Especially this one:

Hearing my husband's car in the driveway, I would run outside to greet him. I could actually feel the warm kiss he would give me.

"Hello, darlin', he greeted me, then turned and reached into the car for a bouquet of red roses.

"Oh, my goodness, they're so beautiful! Come inside and relax. Dinner will be ready in half an hour. Oh, after we eat, I need your opinion on what color to paint the bedroom."

As I turned to go inside to finish readying the meal, he would turn me around, and kiss me hard on the mouth.

He loved me deeply, and I felt so happy to be with him.

Even after coming of age, I missed my sanctuary in the woods. For most of my life, I had built a formidable wall around me that was difficult to penetrate. There, I'd been a prisoner, in a castle of my own making, isolated and afraid. But I couldn't risk facing my fears; I did what came easily, hiding behind them with food, then with amphetamines, and later with alcohol.

A new version of my childhood fantasies continued playing itself out for me as Gene and I pursued one adventure after another, even though, regardless of how I looked on the outside, I remained fragile and easily broken.

Echo

Growing up in the cold climate of New England, I found winter activities delightful. I learned to ice skate on Lake Wampanoag at the end of our street. There was no Zamboni machine in those days. I tripped on the uneven surface, fell down, and kept getting up a million times. And, like riding a bike, it became a skill that some people never let go of.

At the Sculpture Garden in Washington, D.C.

Many years later, Gene surprised me one evening after an early concert at the Kennedy Center, with a detour to the sculpture garden on the National Mall in D.C. It was my birthday, and we were staring at the skating rink.

"You're kidding me, right? I haven't been on a pair of skates since I was a teenager. You want to watch me break my neck?" Genuinely afraid that I had lost the balance and agility I had enjoyed as a child, I shivered in the chill January air and wanted to go home.

"And, anyway, I threw away my skates decades ago."

But, oh, how this man loves to surprise me and throw me off balance.

"Will these do?" he asked, beaming as he handed me a brand new pair of white skates he'd pulled out of his backpack. "Happy birthday, Toots!"

"Oh, Gene, they're beautiful," I gushed. "And size eight: perfect!" Then, I noted mournfully, "Oh, hell, just look at me. I'm not dressed for it."

"Darlin', unless you're stark naked, you can wear whatever you want. And since it's your birthday, maybe they'll let you wear your birthday suit," he joked. "Oh, hell, who's looking anyway? Let's just have some fun on your birthday, okay?" He was unwilling to take no for an answer.

I put on my skates and he rented a pair for himself. With my first glide on the ice, it was as if no time had passed in forty years. First my right leg, then my left, one stride after the other, turning the corners nervously at first and then without effort, gradually picking up speed as my confidence grew. The pop music pumping through the loudspeaker offered Kelly Clarkson singing "Breakaway" as I was trying to let go of my fear and just break away freely—on the ice. By the end of the two hours, I was skating backwards, laughing with Gene as we tried to stay in sync with each other and hold hands. Not one spill that evening, just a sense of wonder and gratitude that there were still lots of surprises and unexpected joys waiting for me around the corner.

And I wouldn't be alone. Gene was sharing the wonder with me.

Gene was a perfect foil for me and my fears. With every "No, I can't," he always scoffed, "Yes, you can." And he liked to have the last word.

When I was little, I'd always wished that things could be different, that I could wave a magic wand and my life would turn into a Norman Rockwell painting. But it never did, and I stopped believing not only that magic would save me, but that anything was magical.

Gene was the magician that evening, and he proved me wrong.

In recent years, Gene has broken both of his wrists while ice-skating. The first time was years ago on that same rink in Washington, D.C. The second time was more recently when we took our grandchildren ice-skating. Putting down the newspaper last month, he called my attention to an article:

"Hey, babe, did you see that Everett has opened a new outdoor skating rink? Let's go do some real skating in the open air like we used to. I really miss the Sculpture Garden back in D.C."

"Sure, that would be so much better than the dreary indoor place we took the kids to in Shoreline. What a difference it will make being outside."

Summit

Being outside. In nature. There's something sublime, almost transcendent, about standing in preserved, natural settings. Getting away from cities and man-made inventions offers a brief opportunity to view the world from God's perspective.

After our misadventure with the hungry bear at Mount Marcy, we drove across the country to the West Coast. Our campsite at the foot of Lassen Peak had inspired Gene to paint again, this time at Lassen and other mountains in northern California in the Cascade Chain. But Gene wanted to go back

At Mt. St. Helens, 2002.

to the site of a recent eruption that had affected the nearby countryside and provided a window into future eruptions for many volcanologists.

On May 18, 1980, in southern Washington near the Oregon border, Mount St. Helens erupted and blew down over two hundred square miles of surrounding forest. There was massive destruction to homes and much of the infrastructure within that area.

Twenty-two years later, Gene and I wanted to view the damage from above. It had become a popular hike for those still hearty enough to make the trek to the top. But this volcano in the Cascade Chain had literally blown its top off two decades earlier. Once 9,600 feet from sea level to the top, it was now 8,300 feet. So . . . less elevation.

It was not Everest—not as high, not as cold, and—when just about everything was for sale—it was practically free to climb, since a climbing permit cost fifteen dollars. But Mount St. Helens was nevertheless a challenge for Gene and me back in 2002. That was the year I quit smoking, but he was still rolling the dice.

Mount St. Helens was as close as I would get to calling myself a "mountain climber." The elevation gain at our base was 3,700 feet, and the elevation gain from where we'd started to where we finished, looking at Mount Adams to the East and Mount Hood to the South, was 4,500 feet, a considerable adjustment in elevation for a couple of adults who'd smoked for over twenty-five years.

Starting out with a leisurely forest walk, we faced a considerable rock scramble. Technically easy but tiresome. "Jesus, Gene, I don't know if I can make it to the top," I complained. "How much more of a rock field is there?" I was sounding like the kid in the back seat on one of my family's long car trips. It took hours to clamber over the regurgitated pumice and rhyolite chunks left on the ground from the eruption two decades earlier.

"Not much more," he assured me. He didn't dare let me know that the rock scramble was the easier part, that trying to ascend through a steep slope of fine ash might be far more challenging. He had done this before and knew what was ahead.

When we finally cleared that rugged terrain, we got to what Gene had avoided telling me about: ash on a steep incline. Very

In the California Cascades.

much like sand, the ashy incline was so steep it seemed that I was taking one step forward and retreating two steps backward. If we were lucky, we approached something to grab onto as we pulled ourselves up the slope. But it was slow going and frustrating.

I'd been in love with Gene for nearly a decade, and I pushed myself to meet him where he was. Not an athletic woman myself, Gene presented a high bar for me to aspire to. His athleticism was so much greater than mine that I struggled to keep up with him. Hiking with his tall, lanky body was a breeze for him. Paddling a fully loaded, eighty-five-pound boat was easy for him. And mountain climbing, though his lungs were challenged, thrilled him as he watched the world disappearing below and moved closer to the open skies. Though I was a willing student, I could never match his ability to glow and thrive in the midst of those challenging activities.

But I was thoroughly committed to Gene. And surprisingly competitive. Though I was a late bloomer, I did the best I could to be an enthusiastic and collaborative partner.

It took eleven hours to complete this hike. Finally, we made it to the top and immediately felt the exhilaration of having worked hard for an achievement. We rested our weary bodies for a bit, took pictures, and turned around to go back down. As I'd been climbing up, I noticed some people on the glacier alongside us shimmying down on saucers—those silver, round, banged-up things I'd had as a kid. Now that I was descending, and feeling it in my knees instead of my lungs, I wished I had carried one of those lightweight saucers on my back.

Barreling down the glacier that way would have been a gas.

Snow in July

On our way home from the West Coast that summer, we took advantage of being in the upper Northwest and its accessibility to a couple more national parks: Glacier National Park near the Canadian border in Montana, and Yellowstone National Park in the northwest corner of Wyoming.

Driving in Gene's pickup truck was slow and tiresome, but that's what made the drive remarkable: hobbling along all of those back roads in our vehicle with a canoe and bicycles on top meant that we had to drive slowly and soak in the scenery. A blessing in disguise. For this East Coast city girl, the summer of 2002 was a revelation: tall, snowcapped mountains with creamy, turquoise, glacial till flowing into the rivers we passed, and acres of meadows, vibrant with colorful alpine flowers. Driving through the Bitterroot Valley was a peaceful, quiet drive off the beaten path, until we reached Kalispell and the entrance to Glacier National Park.

Our first excursion at the park was a hike up to Grinnell Glacier. With a view from above of exquisite, azure Grinnell Lake down below, it was a must-do hike I'm glad I took. I remember gingerly tiptoeing atop the surrounding ice while we took a break, awaiting our descent. Now, with the glaciers melting twenty years later, I wouldn't recommend doing that. But we were with a large group of hikers and felt entirely safe.

The hike back down was uneventful until we reached the last part of the trail going through some woods. Gene and I heard a strange, crackling sound and got nervous.

"Honey," I said, nervously reaching for Gene's hand, "did you hear that loud rustling in the woods back there?"

"Yeah. Just keep moving, and keep your eyes forward," he replied, not sounding particularly worried.

My recent escapade concerning a black bear was fresh in my mind. And I'd seen a number of bear movies, including Anthony Hopkins in *The Edge*, which cured me of ever wanting to be near one. You just can't outrun most bears.

Just as we'd suspected, a grizzly bear was waiting there for the caravan of tourists to pass by. He was discreet, taking cover behind the bushes bordering the trail. We were close to the end of the line, and I turned around, incredulous, to see a full-grown grizzly stroll across the trail and continue on to the woods on the other side. Imagine that: a courteous bear!

Or else he must have eaten well that day.

Gene recalled his first hike along the Grinnell Glacier trail a few years earlier:

The way up to the glacier boasted spectacular lake vistas, and the shrunken glacier itself still reflected its former glory in the glacially carved descending valley. On the way down, I passed a pair of chatty hikers and headed quietly at a brisk pace toward a cathedral-like opening in the woods, beyond which lay a steep incline full of bearberries.

And one big bear. A grizzly. Close. I heard a series of four or five heavy thumps and a grunt or two, and for an instant, framed in the greenery, I saw a grizzly bear in profile, at most twenty feet ahead, trotting to the left on the trail ahead of me, then off into the brush on the downside of the trail.

Heart-stopping.

"Babe, let's put the boat in the water," I suggested the next day. "I really miss paddling, and isn't that why we dragged the Malecite all across the country with us?"

"Of course. I was just waiting for a good opportunity. On the way here, the put-ins were lousy, and I was anxious to get here. Was it everything I said it was?" he said expectantly. Having been to many of the places he was introducing me to, Gene was an informed tour guide, happy to impress me with visits to these remarkable places.

"Yes, darlin'—everything and much more," I assured him, squeezing his hand.

Men have been dazzling women forever: diamond rings, yachts, gorgeous houses, any number of material things. Gene knew how to seduce me: just take me outdoors, the more spectacular the scenery, the better.

Lake McDonald provided the opportunity to put our boat in the water for the first time on that trip. Paddling those pristine waters with snowcapped mountains all around us gave me an intense feeling of peace and contentment. The sanctuary I had always sought—the woods, the mountains, and the water—all there in one place. Glacier National Park was an unforgettable venue to live out our dream for a few days. Before we retired, summers were convenient opportunities for us to retreat into nature and find the solace and peace we needed.

Leaving Glacier, we returned to the southern road, our next stop Yellowstone National Park, a gigantic volcanic caldera at an elevation of eight thousand feet. And fully active, threatening to blow up the world as we knew it.

Whenever you are bored and looking for something to worry about, you can chew on the concept that most geologists believe: the Yellowstone system is way overdue for a big eruption, but maybe not tomorrow. The geysers, Gene explained, were the volcano's way of blowing off steam at regular intervals.

One evening, I was awakened in our tent by the tapping of something on the canvas. Not the hard tapping of a heavy rainfall or the equally hard drilling of hail on the canvas. This was a soft tapping. Of snow. In July.

Stunned by getting stuck in a blizzard in July, half-asleep, half-naked, and shoeless, I grabbed Gene's keys in the attic of the tent, braved the snowfall and scrambled into Gene's pickup truck. I immediately turned on the heater and shivered until the truck started warming up. *What planet were we on where it snows in July?*

"Gene, what the hell? It's snowing!" I yelled as he was approaching the truck.

"Jesus, Marilea, wake up!" he barked at me while putting some things in the truck to keep them dry. "It's over eight thousand feet in the sky here at Yellowstone! What do you expect?" A geyser blowing off his own steam.

"Okay, okay. I hadn't thought of our elevation. Cut me some slack, will you? I'm freezing!" I bristled, hoping for some sympathy and less gruffness.

"Sorry, babe. I'm being an awful bear," he apologized, softening his tone. "Turn off the engine and come back inside the tent. I can think of a few ways to warm you up," he suggested, covering my frozen fingers with his own.

Music in the Desert

The following year, not yet having been to Santa Fe, I wanted to go there. It boasted, among other things, a world-renowned outdoor opera. We got tickets to a performance of *Così Fan Tutte* and flew to Albuquerque in July.

Marilea and Gene at the opera.

After securing our car rental, we sped along Route 25 north to Santa Fe, an hour-long trek in an almost magical setting. Approaching our destination, this fabled town nestled in the Sangre de Cristo Mountains was a welcome sight in an otherwise brown and desolate desert.

We were thrilled to attend our first outdoor opera, set majestically up on a hill in this austere landscape. Experiencing opera in this way—listening to glorious Mozart serenading the close-by hills and villages—was sonorous and uplifting. So much so that, with all the other places left to visit in the country, we returned there for another opera with Gene's sister and brother-in-law two years later.

When I was young and still living in my parents' home, beautiful, classical music was often on the turntable. I especially loved the choral music my father played. Randall Thomas' "The Testament to Freedom," was stirring and powerful. Though growing up in my family had been challenging, fine music was the one thing that helped us cope with the specter of alcoholism. My father, my brother, my sister, and I either sang or played musical instruments and still do to this day. Music helped us, in varying degrees, survive our trying circumstances. Just as it served my family well in the '50s and '60s, it has transformative power everywhere. It can elevate us from where we are on the ground. This is a beautiful thing.

Many people go to church and feel inspired by the moving words of their minister standing before them. They are in their spiritual community. Mine is just about anywhere outdoors where I can appreciate the sanctity of nature. Add beautiful music to the setting, and I feel close to Heaven. This was where Gene and I commune with God: in nature and symphonious music.

When we first started dating, Gene took me to all the dress rehearsals at the Washington Opera where he had been in ticket sales. He bought all the librettos and used to teach me about opera in front of the fire on Saturday nights. I remember learning, for example, how Mozart, who spoke German, sometimes used an Italian librettist, because the Italian language could express the meaning of the story more eloquently. Gene had the opportunity to sing in a couple of operas before I met him, and he was well versed in opera. He taught me a great deal, but he couldn't teach me how sublime the experience would be until I attended a performance.

On our next visit to Santa Fe, we experienced the exquisite voice of Madame Butterfly longing for her child. I was swept away by the poignancy of Puccini's score. Gene's tutelage in opera maximized my enjoyment and appreciation of such a high art form. We were enthralled by the performances at the Santa Fe Opera. The physical setting of the opera house, set high on a mesa overlooking the expansive desert, was stunning.

Not too far down the road, our memories of time in New Mexico would point us back there as we faced a life-changing decision.

God's Work

Our gaze had remained firmly fixed on the Southwest. The following summer of 2004 we took another trip there, specifically to the Grand Canyon, a short drive into Arizona from the airport in Las Vegas.

The magic of the Southwest is in the rocks: the bends and twists, the curves and colors, the sheer durability and splendor. There's so much of it concentrated in this most dry and unforgiving climate that it would take several visits to see all the national and state parks in that area of the United States.

In Gene's rented convertible, we drove north, quickly escaping the glitz of such a big and bustling city. Tired from the long trip, we found a campsite on the park's North Rim, set up the tent, and went to sleep.

Gene always slept in when we went camping, and I was always the first one up to make coffee. But not on this morning. As I opened my eyes, I realized that Gene was already up and had made the coffee for us. What was he up to?

"G'morning, Toots! I've been wanting to show you this since I first came here a few years ago. Put your clothes on, grab your mug, and come with me."

Something had him very excited, and he walked way ahead of me as we headed for his planned destination. I caught up to him and he held out his hand to share with me a beautiful sight: the edge of the park and a view of the canyon as the rising sun was moving over the cliff walls, exposing the colors and textures as it moved.

Gene had been planning this moment for a long time. You know—the way lovers plan sometimes to surprise each other with flowers and candy on an anniversary. This was the kind of man he was, wanting to share one of his best memories with the woman he loved.

I was speechless, remembering these words I'd come across a few years ago by James N. Watkins:

"A river cuts through rock, not because of its power, but because of its persistence."

Since our early separation, Gene and I had enjoyed a steadiness in our relationship. Some might call it stubbornness, but I called it determination. The family issues, the petty squabbles, all the stresses of our lives tested us, of course, but they didn't break the bond between us. They only increased my determination to resolve any difficulties and go on together. I had learned that my practical nature helped him rein in some of his impulses, and that this helped him feel more in control. I was contributing something to Gene that I valued: he, in turn, accepted my gift and adapted accordingly.

"Babe, I'd really like to swing by and see Zion on our way to the airport. I mean, it's not far out of the way."

Trying not to lecture, I appealed to his good sense. "Honey, I know you. As soon as we get to the entrance, I won't be able to drag you away. And we have a plane to catch, remember? Let's save Zion for another trip when we can linger and not feel rushed."

The sun was still low in the sky behind us as we watched the shapes and shadows from it move and rise along the western face of the canyon. You never realize how quickly the sun rises until you see its reflections move across the land. It was a wondrous vision, colorful, and all the more wondrous when you remembered how the canyon had been formed over the centuries.

"We are made to persist," Tobias Wolff wrote. "That's how we find out who we are." Here Gene and I were at midlife, trying not to look over our shoulders at some of the wreckage in our past. We had failed in our marriages to provide secure homes for our children. And still, we persisted.

Though we'd tried to soften the blows—Gene participating in therapy with Patrick, for example, and he and I helping them all go to college—we couldn't take away all their pain. My guilt crippled me for a long time. Being a substance user, I lacked any objectivity, and I continued enabling Annie to ease my anxiety. My work with families of substance users was not sinking in fast enough.

Nevertheless, we had learned about the futility of staying mired in regret. The passage of time and ongoing spiritual recovery would reward us with healthier perspectives on what had occurred before we met. Slow to learn that, we now had to learn to let go of our adult children.

On that day, we were happy together, and we hoped that our love and commitment would propel us ahead toward a brighter future.

Standing at the edge of the canyon, I wiped the tears from my face and absorbed the rapture of that moment in time, my soulmate feeling the same joy and poignancy of God's grace.

Back east, life kept happening, and we needed to pay attention to events as they were unfolding there. My daughter, Annie, was a constant concern for us, and we were doing our best to cope with what was happening to her.

"Honey, I didn't want to worry you," I said, turning to Gene while we waited in the Las Vegas airport for our return flight to Virginia, "but I've been bombarded at home with letters from credit card companies demanding payment. That's one way Annie's been getting cash to buy her drugs—with cash advances. She also stole my identity to get a credit card. I know I have to confront her about this, but God help me, I'm not sure what to do."

Gene said nothing at that point, still absorbing the shock. He was in pain too, careful to hold my hand and support me, but leaving me enough space to figure out how to handle it.

The bomb that exploded in my living room hit us all with its shrapnel.

Music Man

As a teenager, I had a good voice, and my dad encouraged me to sing in various choruses. Gene knew this too, so he enlisted me to be the vocalist in his band.

He was happy to be renting a duplex apartment with a big basement—big enough to accommodate two sets of drums, instruments and people to play music together. He had a number of friends, a couple from the recovery rooms he frequented, and they came over on Sundays to jam.

"C'mon, babe. It'll be much more fun if you sing with us." He was good at cajoling me.

"Are you sure? I don't know all the songs by heart. It's been years!"

"Marilea, who cares if you don't know all the lyrics? You can hum in the gaps. Just sing with us, okay?"

Despite my shyness, those Sunday afternoons hamming it up were a lot of fun. I enjoyed refreshing my memory with songs from the Rolling Stones and The Beatles, and a few of Linda Ronstadt's mournful love songs. But it was Bonnie Raitt whom Gene and I appreciated for all her sexy energy. I glorified her, belting out her raunchy lyrics of "Tangled and Dark," while Gene undressed me with his eyes.

It was exactly where we were in our relationship.

I've always been uncomfortable with silence.

Back in Virginia when I was still teaching, I never drank during the week. I was disciplined about going to work, clear-headed. But on weekends, if I wasn't busy with work or something else, I could get into trouble with alcohol. Even these days, I need to keep busy.

On one Saturday, I had just had a dreadful phone call from Annie. I kept pleading with her to go to another rehab, and she kept telling me she could give up drugs on her own. My first three years in my twelve-step meetings were not helping me, and I was sicker than she was with codependency. By 3:00 p.m., the walls were starting to close in on me and I reached for the wine. I'd finished my second glass by five o'clock when Gene came home.

He saw the wine glass in my hand and me listening to the silence and staring at the wall. He cut through it quickly and went to put on a Benny Goodman record. My doom-and-gloom mood lifted as soon as I heard the music and, a little tipsy, I got up and danced to the music. Gene got out his clarinet and played along. This dance Gene and I have with each other has always lifted me out of a dark space.

Music has that power. It is still the cornerstone of our lives indoors when we're not out and about or walking on the beach. Without music in the background, there's sometimes a deafening silence in our home.

Higher Learning

Year after year, my supervisors had been assigning student teachers to me. I'd been teaching in high school for twelve years, and I felt ready in 2003 to enter a master's program in teaching at George Mason University.

I'd envied my colleagues who went the extra mile to better themselves in the profession, and I wanted to be one of them.

George Mason's was a course designed for teachers working full-time with little spare time. Every moment of those two years was a joy for me. The coursework required a great deal of journaling and writing. From 2003 to 2005, I voraciously read books for my studies that, even now that I'm retired, I still refer to in my writing (and that nine and fifteen years after earning my degree resulted in two published memoirs).

My plunge into graduate school couldn't have come to me at a better time in my life. My daughter Annie was sleeping at my place, on and off, but going through a terrible struggle herself, one with which I couldn't help her.

"Mom, where are you taking the computer?" Annie asked in the basement, indignant.

"I'm in school now, Annie, and I will be journaling and doing papers on the computer. It will stay with me upstairs in my room."

On the last day of our classes, we all gave our presentations before an audience. I worked long and hard on mine, getting the PowerPoint slides put together with an audio background. Gene was taking me to Santa Fe later that day to meet his sister and her husband for a few days of opera and sightseeing. And to celebrate my master's degree.

"I'll see you over there, Gene. Do you remember what room my presentation will be in?"

"Sorry, babe," he called out from his kitchen. "I've got too much packing to go to your presentation. But I know you'll do great. I'll see you back here for lunch and then we've got to race to the airport."

"Okay." I felt disappointed but let it go, kissing him as I went out the door. I knew he would have gone if he could have.

As I was getting my slides ready to put on the screen, I saw him walk into the room and quietly sit down.

He blew me a kiss and aired the greeting, "Break a leg, Toots!"

My heart skipped a beat and I breezed through the presentation. My success that day was my victory, but it was Gene's too. For two years, I'd been immersed in books and writing, with very little free time for him, but he never complained. He always gave me the space to follow my dreams, secure in the knowledge that if it made me happy, we'd be stronger together.

As Gene says:

"Watching you grow as a teacher helped me in innumerable ways. You went through a lot to attain your goals . . . and you succeeded! Your strengths also helped me as we navigated the traumatic times with Annie."

Gene always loved to surprise me with things. He had planned all along to attend the presentation, so the look on my face when he arrived was priceless. That's how we roll, playing off each other for maximum effect. And always with humor, one of his most seductive qualities.

Gratitude filled me up that day. This is who Gene was. He's as sexy and exciting now as he was when we first fell in love.

Greed 101

I could have died, amazed at my abject stupidity, and all for a measly quarter!
Colorado was one of our chosen destinations the following summer. Rocky Mountain National Park lay just to the northwest of Estes Park, a trendy suburb of Denver. After window-shopping a bit and collecting a few more gifts for family and friends, we left the affluence of the area and drove to our campsite in the park. After resting for a day, we started packing for some primitive backpacking. The trash bins, with bear latches, reminded me of the serious menaces around us.

We were near the base of Thunder Mountain, and there was a lake with the same name on top of this peak. Gene had such a fascination for all mountains and how they were formed. The geology of this process. He explained to me how the earth squeezed open from two sides, how it appeared to belch and thrust itself upward, creating the landforms we know as hills, plateaus, sierras, and mountains. It is impressive to discover how the landforms we look at every day were created. I was learning from him how to break out of my complacency, give in to curiosity, and ask more questions. I wondered, for example, about the earth's pull of gravity, and where it was strongest. At sea level, Gene told me, and weaker on mountaintops. Well, I would soon receive a lesson in gravity.

We loaded up our packs with as much forethought and intelligence as we could muster. As always, Gene carried the biggest load for the two of us, easily fifty pounds. I could barely manage twenty-five. All my personal things, of course, plus some of the light, collapsible pots and pans. Fortunately, we didn't have to add to our weight by carrying a lot of water. We were passing clear, running streams all the way up the mountain. But we always disinfected the water with iodine pills and got used to the taste.

Thunder Lake Trail is about eleven miles long and is rated as difficult. The lake itself (10,574 feet) is a popular destination in the Wild Basin. After hiking for about five miles, I felt exhausted and disheartened at how much farther we needed to go. My legs started feeling wobbly and I was tripping along the trail.

"Honey, how much farther is it?" I was needling him again. And perilously close to tears.

Not having fun and feeling the need to keep up with Gene, I tried to push myself through it. It was either that or sit down and not be able to get back up. There, on the north side of the trail, were many backcountry campsites.

Registering my distress, Gene decided to set up a campsite and take the ascent more slowly. This was a good idea; I felt less pressure to keep up and could regain my strength before the next day. As hard as I tried to keep up with my companion, I realized that I was not a young woman anymore—and not for the first time.

"Okay, babe, let's stop here. There's a nice site over there next to a stream. Let's unpack and set up the tent for the night."

I breathed a sigh of relief, threw off my pack, and hugged and kissed him hard.

"Agreed! I'll do better and get more out of it if I take it more slowly."

"Hmmm," he teased. "I have an idea you're gonna love! Help me get the tent up and put on your suit. We're going swimming."

After cooling off in the clean, rushing water, Gene prepared a savory dinner of couscous, and we relaxed in the tent for the rest of the evening. We talked, we serenaded each other with musical memories from jamming with the boys in Virginia, and we held each other captive in the confines of our small tent.

The next day, refreshed and ready for some serious uphill hiking, we made the gradual ascent along the Bluebird Lake Trail. We were rewarded at the top with views of the Continental Divide, Boulder-Grand Pass, Tanima Peak, Pilot Mountain, and the massive Mount Alice.

By that year, 2006, I'd been getting to know the outdoors with Gene for well over a decade. I'd learned what was challenging about going up a mountain, where it hurt (in my lungs), and what hurt going down (my knees). I'd learned how critical it was to pack as little as possible when backpacking. And I'd learned how too much weight on your back could sometimes be dangerous.

Coming back down the mountain a few days later, we stopped on the trail to enjoy the stirring view to the east. It was close to noon and the sun was high over our heads. A reflection at my feet caught my attention, and I saw that it was a quarter, half-covered with dirt.

This particular trail, and many others we'd explored over the years, was not for small children. There was no railing, nothing to protect a person from toppling over to the chasm hundreds of feet below. Care and caution were required. But I threw both to the wind that day.

"Honey, look, someone dropped a quarter! Maybe their change purse sprung a leak and there will be coins, like Gretel's breadcrumbs, all along the trail. How much do you want to bet that I'll find more quarters before we get to the bottom?"

"If you're not careful, you'll get to the bottom sooner than you'd planned. Now I need to pee like a racehorse," he said, wincing in discomfort. "Wait here for me, and forget about the quarter." He left my side for a moment to find a bush.

Well, I did half of what he told me to do: I waited for him. But I didn't forget about the quarter. Without even bothering to remove the heavy pack from my back, I bent over and tried to pick up that quarter. Such a serious lapse in good judgment. Luck was with me then as I lived to tell the tale.

The weight of the pack on my back overwhelmed me and I lost my balance, nearly toppling into a ravine one hundred feet below. I screamed just as Gene caught me and pulled me back from oblivion. Another brush with death—my guardian angel was still with me.

From that day forward, I vowed to never pick up so much as a penny on the ground at my feet—not even a hundred dollar bill.

Surely someone else needs it more than I do.

California Dreamin'

John Muir, known as the "Father of the National Parks," was an early advocate for the preservation of wilderness in our country. It was his activism that helped to save the Yosemite Valley and other large natural areas from the encroachment of wealthy developers. More than once on our trips to the parks, Gene gazed at an untouched area and groaned, "I wonder how long it will be before we see condos there."

A week after our backpacking trip in Colorado, Yosemite National Park beckoned. We were tired from the grueling hike up to Thunder Lake, and we had intended to relax and take in the spectacular views from above. Gazing at Half Dome was a popular pastime, an easy walk from the parking lot. And there was an endless variety of trails, both easy and difficult, to explore. But our time in the park tested us in unexpected ways.

Soon after we arrived, we found a campsite and set up our tent. Maybe we were too tired to notice how crowded the area was right then. We were sandwiched in between two other groups of visitors. The party on our right side was playing loud music way beyond curfew, and Gene, a man who kept his emotions undercover, was fuming.

"Marilea, let's pack up everything now so we can get the hell out of here in the morning."

"Where are we going? We just got here!"

"Down into the backcountry. It's the only way we'll have any peace here. Down there, we can set up the small bivouac tent."

I wasn't exactly looking forward to another ambitious backpacking hike, pots and pans and all. I had just experienced one of them on Thunder Mountain and I was hoping for a break. We looked at the available trails and found one. It climbed down about three miles, which meant we would have to climb back up, still with our pots and pans. But this time, with much less food.

Going down was easy, except for our creaky knees.

"Babe, give me some more of the weight. I'm afraid you'll topple forward with that weight on your back," Gene offered.

"Honey, I'm okay. It'll flatten out soon according to the topo, and then the walking will be easier. Gravity won't be my enemy." *Had I already forgotten about my near spill on Thunder Mountain? Gravity could have killed me there!*

The descent was sharp at first—one switchback after another—but then it leveled off into a resplendent meadow with colorful wildflowers in full bloom. The fragrance was intoxicating, and the warm sun made us feel lazy. We put down our packs and took a long break over lunch. Gene set up a stove, whipped up a simple frittata, and we slowly savored it with some sliced bread and dried honeydew melon.

Lingering on the trail all day wasn't an option, however, since we still had a ways to go to find a campsite. Gene always found the best places to pitch a tent. He studied our map and found a spot in a flat, grassy area with running water flowing in a stream nearby.

For the next two days, we enjoyed the spiritual retreat we'd longed for. I found peace in the silence and we didn't talk much, taking some leisurely hikes and basking in the perfect weather. But on Sunday, we knew we had to go back.

Up.

It was hard work. Gene had not yet given up smoking. Every few feet, he had to stop and lower his head, catching his breath. It took twice as long to get back up to the parking lot.

We were pleasantly rewarded, however, by a stream of back-packers heading down to the valley where we'd been, and maybe for the same reason.

Loudly applauding us as we passed them, they saw us huffing and puffing with grim faces, martyred to the core. Their intention was to congratulate us for our efforts, and we might have been more gratified if we hadn't been so exhausted.

When we made it to the parking lot at the head of the trail, we asked a willing tourist to take our picture.

We looked like death.

"Never again, Gene. I'm not a mountain goat, and I have nothing to prove. I've done enough backpacking for two lifetimes! Just car camping from now on, okay?"

He never answered me.

An Unraveling

It would take more than my lifetime to see all of the national parks. But backpacking in them? I was growing more content to visit the well-worn trails laid out for the tourists. In a car.

But Gene had other plans.

The following summer, one hot July in 2007, we traveled almost as far away from Virginia as you can get on the North American continent. We flew to Vancouver, British Columbia, to climb up Mount Garibaldi in the northern Rockies. Gene had been there before; it was on the way north from Vancouver to Whistler where the Winter Games would be held in 2010. Gene wanted to repeat the 1998 hike, with me, this time.

In 1998, I had gone to Greece to visit my friends. So Gene drove his Ford Ranger across the country by himself to see a few of the parks he would show me later. This was one of those places he loved the most, and he was anxious to share it with me.

On the highway north to Whistler, Gene shouted suddenly, "Stop the car! I want to show you a beautiful lake. Drop-dead gorgeous, jus' like you, Toots!" he said, planting a wet kiss on my cheek.

Well, he was a charmer. But I was the practical one. Mix dreamer with practical and you might just get vinegar . . .

Leaving our rented car in the parking lot of Garibaldi Provincial Park, we set about to climb five miles up to the lake Gene had been referring to. We would set up our tent in the campground, and from there, make the trek up to Black Tusk, a volcanic neck of Garibaldi Mountain.

Gene felt we needed to get far away that summer. The difficult time I'd been having with Annie was proving to be too much to handle. I was fast losing her to the living death of substance use disorder. She had moved from methamphetamine to cocaine and was now addicted to heroin. Nearly at my breaking point, I was falling apart emotionally. I suffered from severe anxiety and insomnia, buried in fear for my daughter.

I felt relieved when school was out that June. I'd been feeling shaky and so tired from the many sleepless nights when Ambien didn't work for me. The joy I used to feel from teaching my students was being sucked out of me, and some days, I could barely teach my classes. Gene was aware of all this as we'd been talking all spring about our summer plans.

"Babe, let's fly to Canada this summer. You've never been to the Pacific Northwest, but remember I went there myself when you went to Greece? I can't describe the beauty; you have to see it for yourself. Let's get tickets and go in July."

"How can I go so far away from Annie again? She's getting worse. Honey, I don't know if she's gonna make it. I feel like I need to be here."

"Yeah? How well has that been working out? Do you think she appreciates your presence in her life? Other than giving her money, what else do you represent? Believe me, babe, I know what I'm talking about. If they're still using, substance users only care about getting the next fix. Maybe she'll come around someday and seriously work on recovery. God knows, I hope so. But I can't stand to see you hanging around for more abuse. The best thing you can do right now is to get away and try to unwind."

I too thought if I could knead the pain out of my heart by climbing a mountain, I might start to feel better. But I was not a skilled mountain climber. The physical challenge facing me now would be considerable. And the spiritual one, even greater.

Fifteen switchbacks: I counted 'em. We were backpacking on an elevated trail. And we had full loads. The trail seemed to go for a mile before it mercifully turned the other way. Would that add up to fifteen miles? Or did it just seem like that? There was only one way to go, and that was up.

After a while, I started fantasizing about being airlifted to our destination: powerful fairies swooping down and grabbing us by the shoulders, bypassing the trail and slicing straight up through the thickly stacked trees, gently placing our grateful bodies down at the campsite and returning to the air without so much as a thank you or a tip.

Then I tripped over a rock and woke up.

This was neither the first nor would it be the last time we were swept away and allowed our good judgment to take a back seat. We began the hike without any planning for food at all. A big mistake. But Gene didn't see it that way. He could withstand hunger and many other discomforts. I was more challenged by the things that didn't bother him. Gene has always tried to help me rise above an immediate problem and see it from another perspective.

What a gift.

"Gene, for Chrissake, we didn't plan this at all! We should have gone shopping first and gotten enough food to sustain us. How are we gonna live on so little protein?" I yelled, already anticipating disaster. My gnawing hunger brought out the worst in me; my character was going to be sorely tested.

"Darlin', when you see the turquoise lake at the top, you won't care," he assured me.

"Yes I will," I moaned, dramatically shaking my head. "Oh, yes, I will . . ."

Every day, when we wake up, life happens to us. We can't escape what comes. How we face it, the choices we make, with or without a problem to wrestle with, is a test of our mettle. On this particular hike, out of the many we had taken, I failed to meet our difficulties with any grace. But—as with most of the mistakes I've made—this one in the Canadian Rockies contained a gem of wisdom to add to the others I've collected over the years. It's a highly recurrent one.

About halfway up, tired, sweaty, and irritable, we decided to lighten our loads by eating our hamburgers. That was a grave error in judgment, cutting down on our food supply so early in the trip. We would dream of eating those hamburgers two days later when we were running out of food and the stamina to keep hiking.

Another mistake was impulsively starting the hike at two o'clock in the afternoon. The only thing that might have saved us in that regard was the lingering light at that latitude in the summer months. But we would be cursed again, this time by the weather: we would not experience any evening lightness.

Gene and I soldiered on. We were too proud to turn around and go back down. I kept thinking of that turquoise lake, and Gene belted out an aria from Samuel Ramey in "Mefistofele."

Not a good choice, but I guess we were wrestling with the devil in some ways. My own dark side was coming out in glossy technicolor.

"Goddamn it, Gene, how could we even attempt this hike without planning better? We could have found a store. What were you thinking?"

No answer.

"Look, I know I share the blame," I continued. "But for God's sake, let's plan better in the future to avoid this sort of thing."

"You're right. I got swept away. But we're here now. Let's try to make the best of things as they are, okay?"

I was mad. At Gene for getting swept away, and at myself for going along.

Five hours later, the sky grew dark, and we knew what was coming. We got caught in a drenching downpour. If I'd adopted a better attitude, I'd have been grateful for the free air conditioning about to cool us off. We were near the end of the trail and had come upon the lake Gene had been talking about. He marveled at it through the trees as he pointed it out to me. But I didn't care. My stomach was growling. And I was soaked. I was in no mood for silver linings.

As we arrived at the campsite and prepared to pitch our tent, we were presented with one: the rain had let up just in time to let us appreciate our elevated spot overlooking Lake Garibaldi and Sphinx Glacier, a gorgeous spot that Gene would photograph multiple times. It's still one of his favorite photographs.

But I was not yet able to distinguish between happiness and joy.

So began three days of wilderness camping and hiking on a subsistence-level diet. It was necessary to ration all of our food.

Ration our food? On a demanding hike in the Canadian Rockies? That's the one thing we should have had enough of. Primitive camping carries with it enough discomforts without adding that to the list. Gene had always added to his own backpack the weight of extra food so we'd never run short.

The next day, we walked around that lake, eating half a sandwich each for lunch. I learned to eat slowly, savoring every morsel. I'd never appreciated gorp so much. Dinner was half-rations again and sleep was fitful. I was ravenous.

We tackled the real focus of our trip on our second day at the campsite: a lengthy trek up to the base of Black Tusk. We made it, trudging all the way up to the snow line. Took congratulatory pictures. Then we went back down with little to look forward to but half a sandwich.

The thing about hunger is, like pain, it's a nasty distraction. Loading up on plenty of filling food every day, like most intelligent hikers, I would have been enjoying the breathtaking views. Instead, I was guzzling water to quell my hunger pangs—and dreaming about food.

The third morning, suddenly finding ourselves humbled—a couple of seasoned backpackers—we asked people for any extra food as they were packing out. They gave us apples, more gorp, and sorry looks.

We were not too proud to ask for help when we needed it. But looking back, it's sometimes necessary to ask for assistance, especially out in the wild. I'm glad we did so and will continue to do so when necessary. We have never, once, in all these years of hiking, been denied help when we asked for it.

Flying down those same fifteen switchbacks the next day, we jumped into the car and sped down the road to a Chinese restaurant in Squamish. Spring rolls the width of thermoses, chicken and this, noodles and that, we gobbled up each dish like it was our last meal. Food had never tasted so good.

I'm certain I've never experienced true hunger or anything even close to starvation. Had I been willing to recognize silver linings in the midst of difficulties, as my partner did, I might have ignored the discomfort and focused on the stunning landscape surrounding me—important food for the soul.

Happiness involves many good feelings and happenings: nice weather, friendly people, a delicious meal. But I have found in my experience that it's necessary to dig down much deeper to access the channels to joy.

On this Canadian hike, the gem of wisdom most shimmering to me was that despite the outward and transitory nature of many things, both pleasant and otherwise, joy from gratitude at having persevered through true difficulty was most profound—and the most salient lesson of all.

The Wrong Boots

By summer 2008, despite nature's sanctuary on our trips, my un-raveling was complete. I felt compelled to take early retirement from my teaching job in Virginia. And regardless of my reasons, this was a time of great loss and mourning for me. In the throes of clinical depression, my vulnerable emotional state surely af-fected my state of mind. Hiking up Black Tusk on nearly empty stomachs would seem like a walk in the park compared to getting swallowed up and spit out on the most strenuous and deadly hike we'd ever taken.

Gene and I had relished going to most of the notable parks in Utah. The state parks are actually much nicer than national parks, because they often come with free showers. And in Utah in the summer, that's a treat to look forward to at the end of the day.

I remembered from a few years earlier standing in line at Grand Teton National Park in Idaho for one hour with my sweaty hands full of quarters, desperate to wash away all the dirt and grime, only to have the money slot for the shower not work. I banged and screamed and tried to dismantle the damn thing that had stolen my money and given me nothing in return. I stomped back to our tent and whined about my misadventure in the showers. *Damn it! I wanted a shower!*

I still don't get what I want a lot of the time—little things mostly, but also heart-wrenchingly big things—but if I have no control over the outcome, I let them go. This was a very small example of the Serenity Prayer at work—"God, grant me the serenity to accept the things I cannot change . . ."

There's a reason why Utah is one of the most magnificent geological wonders in the world: heat and dryness. The rock formations are dazzling to the eye. We've been to a majority of the national parks in the United States, but we keep going back to the parks in Utah. It boasts about forty-five state and national parks in one state. And if you like rocks, it's a visual smorgasbord. The Vermilion Cliffs, for example, located just south of the Utah border, are aptly named for the brilliant and varying shades of red earth. It's quite a sight from the highway.

Canyonlands is one of our favorite national parks in Utah. They're all pretty stellar, but I particularly like Canyonlands because of its camping sites. Camping in thick forests—and getting eaten alive by the insects that have every right to be there—can get annoying. "They have to eat too," Gene would remind me in his most maddeningly teasing tone. So the dryness of the desert combined with the big evening sky was a delightful change from the Northern Woods of Canada and Minnesota.

We headed east from Salt Lake City on a road to Dead Horse Point State Park. Just before the park entrance, we saw a pygmy rattlesnake crossing the road. This was not our first trip to the desert southwest, yet I had never once seen a rattler. But they're there. They just don't come out around people during the day; they come out at night when they do their hunting. At night, rattlesnakes are everywhere, and you don't want to encounter one by surprise.

After we set up our tent at the campsite, we drove over to see why this park got its name. Dead Horse Point is situated atop a high plateau at an elevation of about six thousand feet. From the point, layers of geologic time may be viewed, revealing three hundred million years of the earth's geological history. This is why Gene loves Utah. It was as if God had taken a knife and sliced mountains and chunks of land right down the middle. All the erosion of time could then be viewed for free by anyone who was passing through to see how short the human lifespan was, geologically speaking.

According to the legend, Dead Horse Point was used to corral wild mustangs roaming the mesa. Cowboys rounded up these horses and herded them onto the point. They fenced off the neck with branches and brush, creating a natural corral surrounded by high cliffs. Cowboys then picked the horses they wanted and left the rest to die of thirst within view of the Colorado River, two thousand feet below. I hoped some of those horses had the good sense to leap over the brush to their deaths and die quickly.

Death was the last thing on our minds the next day. We woke up bright and early, ready to enjoy our last day in Utah at a leisurely pace. Why did I put on my winter-weight hiking boots? Well, I didn't have any lightweight boots. I only had the Merrell's Gene had bought me back in 1994 so that I'd have more ankle support. After all the hikes we'd been on, from Thunder Mountain to Yosemite to Garibaldi, to name a few, it surprised me that my feet hadn't suffered more from the constant pounding of my toes inside my winter boots. But my luck was about to change.

That day, in particular, I wasn't planning on doing any serious hiking at all. It started out innocently enough; the various trails were outlined on a billboard.

Upheaval Dome/Crater View

Round trip	2.5 mi (4 km)
Elevation gain	300 ft (91 m)
Hiking time	15 minutes to 1 hour
Difficulty	Easy

Piece of cake—a relaxing walk along the rim of this crater on a typically hot day in July. It was too hot to do anything more exerting that day. We thought we'd start the day with this little stroll to view the inside of the crater. Then we'd take the car farther south around the Needles District. Even though dry heat was much easier for me to tolerate than sweltering humidity, we were still pretty tired from a week of hiking. This would be our "wind-down" day, a day to decompress before we hightailed it over to Salt Lake City to catch our flight back to Virginia.

Pulling into the parking lot at 10:00 a.m., we got out of the car and studied the billboard at the start of the hike. With the whole day to kill time, we could dawdle. In our fanny packs were about two bottles each of water and the usual munchies I always carried to fend off hunger. We also packed a lunch, since all our food was back at the campsite and we knew we'd be gone until dinner. Luckily, the same guardian angel that kept me alive on many other occasions was watching over us that day: instead of leaving the lunch on the front seat, we carried it with us. We had no idea that because of our overconfidence and lack of preparedness, we would soon be swallowed up by this crater we had intended to observe only from above—and were lucky to get out alive.

The guidebook distinguished between the easy, Crater View walk (above) and the actual hike into the Syncline Valley, which was rated as "very difficult:"

"Be prepared for a hike as demanding as it is dramatic," the guidebook warned us about going into the Syncline Valley. "Expect the initial descent and subsequent ascent to be steep and rugged, though both are brief. The ascent is on a particularly rough route, mildly exposed in two places where a burst of gymnastic effort is necessary to avoid an injurious fall. Alleviate these difficulties—plus gain the benefit of some timely, post-exertion shade—by looping clockwise. The counterclockwise hikers we've met here were distressed . . ."

Well, this helpful book, which we hadn't fully read yet, was in the car. We hadn't planned on taking this hike at all, and we were woefully unprepared for a grueling hike on a blisteringly hot day in July. I was wearing the wrong boots.

We took the easy walk up to the rim described in the guidebook and on our way back to the car thought, *Hmm . . . not much of a challenge there. It's only eleven in the morning. Let's be adventurous and see where the trail to the left leads.*

In the Syncline Valley outside of Moab, UT, 2008.

Gene and I were big risk-takers. Some of the risks I'd taken with him were thrilling, like running rapids in Canada when we were too tired to portage. And some were stupid and self-destructive, like taking up smoking soon after we met with his brand, Camel non-filtered, so that we could share.

So we took the trail to the left and began the counterclockwise loop. As we were nearing the valley floor, we met hikers on their way back who saw we were "distressed." And we were only two hours into the loop.

Just like Mount St. Helens, but at least the rock climb here isn't vertical.

"How much farther?" we asked them as we were struggling through some boulders.

They looked at us like we hadn't read the book—which we hadn't—and offered, "Oh, you've got a ways to go. Might have been easier to go clockwise."

Thanks, pal. I already figured that out, I thought, realizing how the sun would face and torture us all along this counterclockwise loop.

Moving on, boulder after boulder, we finally reached the floor of the canyon. At least we weren't fighting gravity at that point.

"Gene, we should have asked them for some water," I complained, already starting to project disaster and panic as I sneaked a peek to the left and saw where we needed to be before the sun went down. *Oh, shit, all the way up there?*

"Don't worry. We're doing fine," Gene said, trying to shut me up and allay his own growing fears that we had gotten in over our heads. I had a veritable Star Wars battle going on inside of me: good versus bad. Bad represented the way I had learned to think for most of my life before I got into substance use recovery: closed-mindedness, pessimism, ingratitude, and above all, fear and panic. The last two used to drive me into caves of denial, avoidance, and ultimately, despair.

We were soon to confront a situation that would require a serious change in attitude on my part. I didn't, however, rise to the occasion that day. I found myself falling into that familiar cave and trying to take Gene with me.

The walk along the canyon floor seemed endless, but I was grateful for the shade of the cottonwoods. Gene was distracting himself by studying the Chinle Formation on the banks of the wash that snaked all along the valley floor. Mercifully, it was dry, or we would have been further challenged.

Straight ahead in seven miles was the White Rim Road, and three miles before that was a campsite. But we had no provisions, no tent, nothing to comfortably make it through the night. All we could think about was getting back to our car as we neared the seemingly sheer cliff we would need to scale.

It was at this point that I turned into a harpy of major proportions. My mother needled my father relentlessly to quit drinking during their marriage, and those nasty tapes found their way to my vocal cords in magnificent stereo.

"Gene, for Chrissake, what are we gonna do? It's seven o'clock already! How could you get us into this mess? We've eaten all of our food, we're almost out of water, and we have a fucking mountain to climb! In two hours, it'll be dark, and of course you didn't bring any headlamps. Did I leave anything out, Sherlock?"

I was shaking with fear and panic. No need to look up at the cliff; we were at the base of it and in its shadow. It was a long way to the top and the sun would be going down soon. It didn't help to see the shed skin of a huge rattler on the side of the path. I knew there were snakes in canyon country, deadly ones. And they came out at night when most intelligent campers were roasting marshmallows around a campfire.

Gene is different from me temperamentally. He usually keeps it all in. The more I continued hammering away, the more his fear and rage built up inside. At some point as we were silently putting one foot in front of the other, he took off in another direction. He just snapped. And he was carrying the water—all of it.

"Gene! Come back here! Where the fuck did you go? You bastard! You have all the water!"

Listening for his footsteps, I stayed on my path, cursing him every few minutes, wishing I had worn a megaphone. I finally gave up yelling, convinced he felt no remorse for leaving me in the lurch to make it out on my own.

This is where the rubber hit the road for me. This is where I drew on my own strength. Gene's impulsiveness had been infrequent over the years, and on many occasions it was fun. But this was where I saw the potential for danger, and I knew I would have to help him manage it better.

I wish I could have looked over my left shoulder at the brilliant sunset and enjoyed the shadows and colors moving across the rocks, transforming their shapes as they went. But on this day, sunset meant dusk was coming, a very tricky kind of light, followed by darkness. My adrenaline kicked in and I was on a mission to survive. I channeled all my rage into a fierce determination to get off that mountain and return unscathed.

Well, return, at least.

Thank God for cairns—small piles of rocks placed at regular intervals, marking a pathway to show hikers where to go. I don't remember when darkness set in, but I do know that those cairns saved my life—the cairns and enough common sense to keep going up instead of across. I think Gene was doing that to find an easier way out.

Or maybe he just needed to get away from me.

I toiled my way up, following the trail marked by the cairns. Ignoring the pain in my legs and feet, moving forward and up was my only option. I had no water and was terribly thirsty, but I just kept going, snaking my way up the switchbacks that seemed endless, until I finally reached the crest of a hill, and I hoped that the worst was over.

Walking through a juniper grove, I saw a hiker approaching me and asked him for some water. He gave me a whole liter, for which I was grateful, and I didn't even ask him why he was going into the Syncline Valley at that hour. It was 10:00 p.m. I made it, refreshed, into the parking lot and flagged down the last car that was leaving. Gene also had the keys to the car and the phone. I asked the people in the car to call Canyon Rescue to come get Gene off the mountain. Thank God someone was in the parking lot to make that call. Silver linings . . .

Now I was in the mood for them.

I lay on the cool linoleum floor of the public bathroom waiting for the squad to arrive. They went right in with whistles and an hour later they came out with Gene. He was too dehydrated to walk, had been drinking his own urine, and had just been sitting there in the bushes, waiting. Thankfully, he hadn't passed out and could respond to the whistles.

When I saw them bring him down I ran to him in relief. But those feelings were short-lived as the enormity of our mistake sank in. I forget how long it took for six of my toenails to loosen and fall off, the result of battering my toes repeatedly inside unventilated boots.

The Garibaldi hike was admittedly a misadventure of sorts. And there have been a few others. But in all the years that we'd hiked together, I have rarely known Gene to be anything less than assiduously prepared, to the point of dragging every topographical map we might need, extra food and water, extra clothing, first aid, and extra books. But anger, panic, and poor judgment got the better of us both in the Syncline Valley.

So often our adventures have just been staging grounds for learning about ourselves. On this trip, I managed to come out a hero. Instead of passively collapsing in fear, I summoned my own resources to get off that mountain. My next priority was to save Gene.

That summer when I forced myself into early retirement was a terrible, low point in my life. But if leaving the classroom could be regarded as a weakness, then it was gratifying to learn that I could find the strength to usher us both through that challenge on the mountain.

We were silent in the car all the way back to the campsite. It would be safe to say we were in shock from our experience. But I hated Gene that evening, and I wondered how I would be able to sort it all out in my mind and return to the comfort zone we had been enjoying.

I sat at our picnic table while Gene got into his sleeping bag and went to sleep. Then I moved my sleeping bag away from his and fell asleep right away.

I didn't wake up until noon the next day. When I awoke, I saw him staring at the attic in the tent. I sat up, then he did, and we looked at each other and reached for each other's hands. Words I had never heard from him spilled out of his mouth. Gene accepted full responsibility for a horrendous lapse in judgment by leaving me alone without water.

"God, Marilea, I'm sorry. I can't believe I acted like that last night. His blue eyes were filled with remorse. "Can you ever forgive me for running off like that?"

I too was able to see my part in our disastrous communication that day and I took full responsibility for pushing Gene to the edge.

"Well, I hated you last night, I really did. I saw a side of you I didn't want to live with. But in fairness, we both acted badly. I gave in to my fear and panic, as I often do. And I was ugly, lashing out at you the way I did. You're not a saint; you reacted. I'm just grateful that I was able to get out and call for help before it was too late."

Though sincerely expressed, these were just words. Time would tell if Gene would be able to control his impulsiveness. Or if I would find the restraint to govern my tongue better. We fell back into an embrace and lay silent for a long time, lost in our thoughts.

I was certainly wearing the wrong boots on this trek, and I lost my toenails because of it. But that was a small price to pay for what I found from the experience.

We were still the right fit for each other.

Gene and I bring out each other's strengths. When he fell short on the mountain, I became the strong one. When my mood darkens, he tries to make me smile. I don't like to cook, so he's been feeding me well all these years. Many times in our years together, we've filled in each other's empty spaces.

I'm at home with him. I can unravel and be myself with him. I can find myself and lose myself and know without a doubt that he'll still be there when I find myself again. On this trip, we saw ourselves at our very worst. And though the dark side took over in both of us that day, we survived to savor the lesson—and each other.

How can I calculate all the gains we've made in our years together?

Loss, Not Quite

Or take measure of the incomparable losses?

From the start of my separation from her father, Annie retreated into periods of depression not unlike what I lived with most of my life. And, not surprisingly, Annie chose the same means as her mother to combat the feelings of sadness that had often overwhelmed her: substance use. The weekly therapy we provided for her didn't seem to help. In the course of those horrible years, our family rallied around her through four rehab facilities, fought to save her in emergency rooms, and when it no longer became productive to remain in contact with her, let her go.

Out of the blue while Gene and I were sitting outside, a call came recently from an old neighbor of mine in Virginia. Her daughter and Annie had been close friends when they were little and they'd played together often. My friend and I had been in touch by email, but not for many years. I flinch, recognizing her voice. *I need to catch up with her, but what will I say about Annie?*

"I'm sorry, but I have to ask," my old acquaintance queried over the phone, her voice tipping me off that she was nervous. "You hadn't talked about your kids much in your emails. How's Annie? What's she been up to?"

Maybe she knew; maybe she'd gotten wind of it from someone else and wanted to hear it from me. If that was the case, then I was feeling ambushed.

Okay, here goes . . . "I'm so sorry, Gillian. The news about Annie is bad and is bound to shock you. Maybe you should sit down. She's been lost in the underworld of substance use disorder for a number of years now, half Annie and half someone else. After twenty years—on and off—of using methamphetamine, cocaine, and heroin, her personality has changed so much that she bears little resemblance to the daughter I raised, the little girl you knew. Now she is living a very different life.

"She was once a competitive gymnast, representing her team in England while we were in the Foreign Service. Didn't she send Tamara a postcard from Greece? She was on the Dean's List one year at American University and continued to do well enough in her classes to graduate from George Mason University in 2004. She was such a thoughtful daughter, never forgetting a birthday or Mother's Day. I have drawers full of her remembrances."

I imagined my acquaintance's eyebrows starting to furrow; she didn't see how all this wonderfulness could have been replaced by something much darker.

I told her that substance use disorder is a cruel thief—cruel because it often "kills" you before it actually kills you.

Many people don't get it. How would they, without living through it themselves?

Tamara's mother remained silent, so I went on.

"The Annie who played with your daughter isn't here today. She cut off all ties to her family years ago, refusing any contact with us. Every few years, she forgets her promise to erase us from her life, and then sends me a series of scathing, raging emails about what a miserable childhood she had. I would like to think it's the drugs talking, yet I can still feel shaken by her ranting. I love her so, my poor, lost girl."

Still no response, so I continued.

"Every year on her birthday, I email her that I love her. And then I let her go, all over again."

I detected a faint blowing sound on the other end of the phone.

"I'm so sorry, Marilea. I had no idea what you've been going through all these years. I'll certainly keep you in my prayers. I've got to run now, but let's stay in touch," she said, quietly hanging up.

Gene stepped in after the call. I was visibly shaking after recounting the nightmare once again. He could see how upset I was. "Marilea, stop it. You did the best you could with what you knew at the time. Annie knows how to get her life back if she ever wants to. Now let it go. Your other kids and grandkids will benefit from a healthier you. And so will I."

"Well, I'm awfully glad Gillian didn't ask for details about Annie's 'other life.' She's had enough shocks for today."

I still harbor a mother's hope that the daughter I brought into this world and raised to adulthood will come back . . . somehow.

My whole life is a miracle. Maybe God, or a stranger on the street, will smile on her.

That's all. This isn't a story about Annie, but of Gene and me and our love for each other. He has been my rock throughout all these years of losing Annie to this slow death.

So much time lost. Unimaginable assaults on her character, all in the interest of serving her new master. I must accept the unacceptable reality that I cannot save my daughter from her disease.

Sometimes I wonder, even after doing recovery work to try to cope with that reality, how I've managed to come out of the darkness intact. I almost didn't. For quite a few years, I stubbornly clung to survival in any way that I could—eating when I was lonely, downing pills when I was sad, drinking to mask the guilt—unaware of the need to save myself first.

Part Four:
SECOND ACTS

"I am not afraid of storms for I am learning
how to sail my ship."
—Louisa May Alcott

Life on Life's Terms

My drinking escalated as Annie's illness worsened. It must have been hard for Gene to keep his mouth shut about my drinking, but he did, and flawlessly, for most of our years together. Many triggers could set me off, but later on, watching Annie abuse her body so badly, it seemed as though I was trying to join her. With every crisis that knocked at my door, I wanted to drink more.

By 2006, Gene had moved into my condominium with me in northern Virginia. His daughter, Bridget, and her roommate needed a place to live, so they moved into his place and he moved into mine. This was a sacrifice for Gene. He liked his house right up the road from my condo. It had a yard to move around in and a basement for jamming. Gene and I would both miss our Sunday music sessions. But he always had a good time playing the guitar with Patrick, who was still living in the area.

All my children had finished college and had spread their wings. Caroline lived in San Francisco, and Carter was about to leave for Austin to get his master's. But Annie was still living in the area, utterly transformed by her substance use disorder. I bore witness, close-up, to unbelievable changes in her character, shocking new behaviors, as I experienced a mother's bewildering sadness and grief. I felt sometimes like going to bed and staying there.

Exploding into my living room a year later with a pit bull and an overflowing suitcase, her eyes were blood red as she pleaded with me.

"Mom, help me. I can't do this anymore!"

Of course I'll help you, my darling girl. We'll arrange for another rehab, and I know it will work this time.

"Annalise," I told her without giving her a choice, "I'm taking you to Arlington Hospital. They can help you there. Where is your car? How did you get here?"

"My car was stolen. I got a ride here," she said, looking toward the door, wild-eyed. "Please get me out of here. I need help."

"Honey, it'll be okay," I offered. "I'm sure they'll give you something to calm you in the hospital."

Thank God Gene was living with me then and happened to be home.

"Gene," I said, trembling, "you need to take Dante to the animal shelter in Alexandria. I'm sure they'll find a home for him." I wasn't sure of that at all, but it helped Annie say goodbye to her dog.

I got in the car with her and drove the short distance away, illegally parking right at the entrance. The staff checked her in to the psych ward. As I turned to leave, Annie suddenly approached me, panicked. Of course she was afraid. She was putting herself in a situation where she would have to stop abusing drugs as long as she was there.

"Annie," I said, warmly offering her a hug, "Gene and I will visit you every day. And Dad and Paula will come over from Georgetown too. Just try to get better. We all love and miss you so much."

She turned away from me and followed the nurse. The door to the psych ward slammed behind her. It only opened in one direction. She was locked in.

And I was locked out. I still couldn't accept the fact that Annie was a runaway train—and I couldn't stop the wreckage. It was October 2007, my favorite time of year. But I was blind to the autumn beauty all around me. The world appeared bleak and colorless.

After I got home, I repeated Psalm 23 over and over again: "The Lord is my shepherd, I shall not want . . . Yea, though I walk through the valley of the shadow of death, I will fear no evil . . ."

I was praying as hard as I could. But not hard enough.

Total Wine wasn't far from my condo. I popped in there for an economy-sized bottle of Chardonnay, not even waiting for the change. The twist-off cap let me start right there in the parking lot. Once again, I felt rattled and sick with worry. Alcohol was how I was finding my courage more and more in those days. The courage to watch my daughter fall into the rabbit hole of substance use disorder and be helpless to stop her.

Mirror, mirror . . . I was following her down that hole.

By the time Gene returned from taking Annie's dog to the shelter, I'd finished about half of the bottle, was terribly drunk, dizzy, and sprawled on the sofa, wailing out loud.

"I'll never do this again, make me promise! This is the last time!"

Gene just held my hand.

Moving On

At the New Mexico/Arizona border.

Gene has partnered with me throughout the trauma of watching Annie succumb to this disease. Under the influence of so many dangerous drugs, she was nearly unrecognizable. He has helplessly stood on the sidelines as I rode the roller-coaster of her illness.

He lived through the sleepless nights. He observed me, worn-out, going to work every day. As always, he cooked for us every night, but eventually I couldn't swallow food and developed crippling intestinal problems. I was losing too much weight and he was alarmed. That's when he put his foot down.

"Marilea, you can't go on like this. Please make an appointment with a psychiatrist right away. You need to talk to someone, and in the meantime, there must be some medication that will help your appetite come back."

I agreed to get help and began to see a doctor every week. His diagnosis was clinical depression. The antidepressant he prescribed, Zoloft, had an immediate positive effect on my physical symptoms, and I began eating normally. But it would take me a long time—years—to continue working through my grief.

Against my psychiatrist's advice, I took early retirement from my teaching job. I was grieving more than Annie. I knew I would miss the rush and satisfaction of teaching. To ease myself out of the field, I wrote a proposal for a two-year project in the department where I'd been working. It was accepted, and I began work right away. I was delighted to be doing work that would keep me collaborating with my fellow teachers. Having left my job so precipitously, I felt like a failure, and the work gave me a sense of purpose and value, something I was sorely missing at that point. My psychiatrist agreed.

Soon after the new year in 2009, I became the impulsive one. Angel and I had spent a great deal of our money putting Annie through four rehab facilities, and I decided to spend some serious money on myself. Gene wholeheartedly agreed, so we pooled our resources and bought a little house in Rio Rancho, New Mexico, one weekend in February. It was meant to be our "second home," but no sooner had we signed the papers than Gene decided to empty out his storage unit, and with the help of his son, move to New Mexico the following month.

I knew how much he adored the open spaces and sunniness of the Southwest. I also knew how much he disliked living in my claustrophobic little condominium with no yard to roam around in. So he jumped at the chance to live in the Southwest. He had retired from his full-time teaching job the year before I did, but continued to teach GED in the evenings. I agreed to teach his classes for him—*we've filled in each other's spaces*—so nothing was holding him back.

We had learned early on to respect, even celebrate the distances we sometimes created from each other—as we did when we were together but chose to live separately for most of our years in northern Virginia. That gave us room to grow as whole and valuable human beings in our own right. And when we bridged those distances, we were stronger for it, both individually and together.

One summer, for instance, while I was taking teaching courses, Gene and Henry went to Ontario to paddle the Bonaventure River.

The Canoe

Love will give you wings to fly.
Faith will never ask you why.
Love will set you free to roam.
Faith will bring you safely home.

—Marilea to Gene, spring 1995

We found that same integrity when Gene left for New Mexico. Growing as we did, both separately and together, was risky, but we crossed the divide with our relationship intact, happier and stronger.

So we agreed to start over in New Mexico, though I would keep the condo in Virginia. This would be quite a change for us. We'd traveled around the United States and seen some remarkable places. But I'd never thought about permanently up-rooting myself.

I'm a New Englander from "Baastin." Gene, too, is an East Coast survivor, quite used to big cities, noisiness, traffic, and self-important people. At this juncture, though, we needed a radical change, looking for more open spaces to move around in, and less of a pressure cooker to live in.

"Will you miss me, honey, out there in the desert with no one to keep you warm at night? I hear that nights can get chilly, even in the summer, at five thousand feet."

"Of course I will. But I have to do this. After three years of living in the condo, I need to have more space. And the house comes with a half-acre of wild sagebrush. I've contacted the school system in Rio Rancho and can substitute in the schools there every day if I want to. You can too when you get there. I know you miss being in the classroom, and it'll be a good source of income for us."

"But what about us now? How will you manage without seeing me every day?"

"Remembering times like this," he said, taking my hand and leading me upstairs to the bedroom. We made love to each other for a long time, no doubt feeling the intensity of it more as we faced our separation.

I would stay behind in Virginia for the remaining fifteen months to finish up my contract work. We planned to go back and forth often to be together, an important choice to keep us connected. But I never made an issue of his moving to New Mexico before me.

Except for one thing.

After he got there, he decided to clear the land, buy fruit trees, and start an orchard.

But he didn't tell me.

"I wanted to surprise you," he deadpanned after my first visit. "I thought you'd be delighted."

"Well, I would have been," I retorted, "if I'd had any interest in gardening."

But I didn't. Hardly at all.

Gene even studied to be a master gardener soon after he moved there. He learned about planting trees in the sandy soil of New Mexico. Aware of the difficulties he'd be encountering, he was undaunted; the challenge excited him.

So the orchard became Gene's bailiwick for the next ten years. I helped a little, and especially enjoyed selling our fruit with him at the open markets where we made friends and listened to the local, raucous bands.

This was his accomplishment, a considerable one. His peaches won more than one blue ribbon at county fairs, and we had so much fruit we had to give it away to food banks and churches. Then sticky, stewed peaches spewed all over the stove and got stored in the freezer. And dried in the food drier. Gene loves peaches. He'd probably try to grow them in Alaska.

We chose New Mexico because we'd been there twice before—to experience an outdoor opera, enjoy the spectacular hiking trails, and witness the still-vibrant Native American culture. That would be a monumental change in lifestyle for us both. But Gene couldn't get out there soon enough. My companion joyfully transplanted himself into sunny New Mexico, a change that thrilled him.

Also, after a lifetime of muggy weather, the dryness was a relief for us. The whole East Coast is a swamp from Maine to Florida. You can't escape the humidity. Maine is chilly and wet; Florida is hot and wet. But it's always been wetter along the eastern seaboard. Gene and I delighted in the ever-present sunshine in the Southwest. But, not surprisingly, all that sunshine scorching the earth and the people living there brought new challenges to the unsuspecting visitor.

It's hard to know the great Southwest until one has lived there and felt the dryness in his bones. Or, after I'd lived there a while, the skin cracking on my ankles where Gene bandaged my bleeding sores. Until I'd seen the monsoon sky and prayed that the clouds would open up and spill out buckets of water to nourish the parched soil. Or, if I'd ever taken a leisurely stroll in one of many slot canyons, seen the darkening sky and listened for the rumbling noise getting louder, frantically scanning the canyon walls for a way out before I became part of the meat grinder moving fast enough to flush me away.

In recent years, drought and disaster for many of the crops have crippled the whole area and other parts of the country. Partly because of the changing climate, and partly because of the sandy soil, Gene's dream of having a fruit orchard—one that he babied every day like a growing child—would become one relentless difficulty after another.

There are few things in life that he salivates over more than a fresh bowl of fruit. Gene was determined to grow the most succulent peaches the grower's market had ever seen.

He came close.

Peaches

And where do I fit in, where is my
    zone of comfort?
    In my orchard, near new growth,
    under the brow of the mile of mountain,
    red mountain, now, and again, at dusk.
    In the stony backyard
    pulling weeds and
    coddling the border xerics
    and the old roses
    making music or best of all—beside you
    co-existing

Simply Being
    with you here physically
    as tangible as the loving you
    that lives within my heart
        spirit
    up there between my ears, I
        can't
        get you outta
        my mind . . .
—Gene, July 2009

When I think of all the times of late
That my busy jangled mind
Shifts down and off to one side

Or the other
Happily distracted by images of your softness
Smiling and glowing warmness,
Torrential downpours tame themselves and
A deep serenity looms prevailing timeless,
Yet tangible, in your kiss.
Lord help me, I miss you.

—Gene to Toots, September 2009, living alone in New Mexico

The Big C

In December 2009, Gene pissed red—and paid attention. Two months later the pathology report came back: Gene had an "asymptomatic, highly aggressive, highly recurrent" form of bladder cancer. That was twelve years ago, so he's safely passed the ten-year mark.

Two things made him one of the lucky ones: first, he had a symptom, blood in his urine; the second thing was that he discovered it at Stage One. Stages matter. The statistics don't lie. Late-stage cancers are often a death sentence. Even with all the new treatments, they sometimes just extend the time you have left.

Gene had a friend who had the same cancer with no symptoms. By the time he was diagnosed, it had moved to Stage Four. Mike eschewed all traditional treatments, preferring to try holistic therapies. He did not die easily or peacefully. Gene and I went to Mike's memorial in New Mexico. His wife needed tranquilizers to get through the ceremony, and her brother had to hold her up.

My contract job would be up by the summer of 2010, but I flew there beforehand to support Gene when he found out he had cancer. He was holding up as I expected him to, uncomplaining and optimistic that he would beat it. Then, that summer I moved there permanently, in time to be there through his cancer therapy.

A few people diagnosed with early-stage bladder cancer are encouraged to undergo an unusual treatment called Bacillus Calmette-Guerin (BCG) therapy. BCG is used to stop the growth of bladder cancer and keep it from returning.

Gene endured his BCG treatments with grim determination, stoicism, and bravery. And I was so relieved to toss out the catheter that felt like such an assault on his bodily functions. Gene wasn't ready to go just yet. What was his secret? Green tea and broccoli sprouts. And "a hunka hunka burnin' love."

All the predictable disruptions and petty quarrels that were part of the fiber and design of our lives together were one thing, but getting a life-threatening illness brought the fragility of life into clearer focus for us. Gene had his own story of fear and coping with the sword of Damocles lingering over his head.

I remember getting up in the middle of a December night to pee, turning on the light above the toilet, and relaxing as I emptied my bladder. My aim is pretty good, especially in cramped quarters, and I recall I didn't look down until I had finished the business at hand. When I glanced at the bowl, my first reaction was a scary one. I thought I had sliced my penis wide open, somehow without pain. The bowl was red with blood. Bright red.

I wasn't sure how to react. *This should hurt.* But no. I experienced no discomfort at all. So I went back to bed. The bleeding was not constant. I saw no problem the next day. But after two days, the bleeding returned. After consulting with nonmedical friends, I made some calls, finally contacting the one urologist in Albuquerque who could see me before six months elapsed. Dr. Martinez was a godsend, with an opening that week.

I went in for the appointment and he "scoped" me in the office. His first words were "How soon can you get to the hospital?"

I responded, "At once," and we arranged for a full-blown procedure to remove a spot on my bladder. Nothing had penetrated the inner wall, it turned out, and whatever the growth was, Dr. Martinez got it all.

"I'll send this to the lab. We'll know within ten days what you've got growing."

Ten days later, I went to his office. There were only the two of us—Marilea was with me in New Mexico after I found out. He looked at me and said, "It's cancer." I looked around the office. Who was he talking to? *Oh, shit. It's me!*

The view from the top of the hill watching my darling make sure he has enough broccoli sprouts every day, hearing his tale of enduring his urologist's twice-yearly "scoping" to make sure the Big C hasn't come back: it's not as tough as having cancer, but it's not easy. Twelve years ago, it was most uncomfortable for him at first to get a tube with a flashlight stuck up his penis every week. Not painful, but surprising. Gene has now graduated to biannual scoping, and handles all the stress and uncertainty with grace and absolute faith that all will be well.

Maybe it's because we're both getting older with new aches and pains to add to the old ones, but every year he's been cancer-free is a year I grow to value and appreciate him more. And I tell him so. I could lose Gene at any time. Who knows? He could lose me to something that hasn't approached yet as I get older. And that knowledge brings our relationship into sharp focus.

Why wait? Gene tells me he loves me every time we part and come back together. And I do the same.

"I love you!" he tells me every time he leaves the house, with a kiss on my mouth.

"I love you more!" I answer, returning his kiss. His eyes twinkle hearing that.

Pure corn, I know.

I hope when death comes to get me, I will greet her with the same gratitude and grace that I try to live my life now. And above all, grateful for the last twenty-nine years with a man who truly loved me and I him. How blessed I've been in that regard.

An asymptomatic, highly aggressive, highly recurrent form of bladder cancer . . .

Gene's cancer has not returned since his treatment in the summer of 2010. Aside from regular checkups with his urologist, no more BCG therapy. We are deeply grateful for this good fortune, and have both vowed to make the most of our years left together.

Waves

Cancer has a way of keeping people on their toes and alert. Gene's family and friends made sure he knew how much they loved and appreciated his presence in their lives. Soon after he finished his treatment, we played host at our house in New Mexico to all of his family members, one after the other: his sister, Susan, and her husband, Jim, came from California; his brother, Michael, and Michael's son, Jesse, drove to New Mexico on their way to Washington State; and his brother, Chris, and his wife, Genny, also flew in. It was a poignant way to reaffirm what really mattered to us. And for Gene, that would be family and old friends.

Henry and Pam were still living in New Jersey, but we all missed the times we had spent hiking and boating together. So much had occurred in all our lives in the intervening years. Henry had had a stroke: healthy, active Henry. He and Pam were able to visit us in New Mexico soon after Gene got cancer. That whet our appetite to tackle a new adventure we could all handle in the Southwest.

"Hey, Gene," Henry said on the phone. "Pam and I have been wanting to go see The Wave for years now, but there's a tight lottery. The officials only allow a certain number of people into the area. Sort of like the canoe situation at Quetico. Would you guys be interested in meeting us there so we can do it together? Pam's taking a week off from work, so we'll have plenty of time."

The Wave, in the northern part of Coyote Buttes—sandwiched in between Vermilion Cliffs National Monument and Paria Canyon, just over the Arizona border—is famous for being one of the most extraordinary rock formations anywhere in the world. Gene didn't need time to think about it.

"We're game. Send us some dates and we'll make it work," Gene answered. It was 2012, two years after his cancer diagnosis, and it was important to Gene to see more of his oldest friend.

The write-up told tourists that if they forgot their cameras, no one would believe their descriptions of what they saw.

"Sounds like *Sergeant Pepper's Magical Mystery Tour.* Sure you weren't on pot the whole time?" a friend chortled at my excited recounting of our trip.

"Jeannie, no, I never smoke pot. Seriously, I thought I'd seen rock formations before. But this place was visually overwhelming. I'll let my pictures show you. Words won't do it justice."

Because of The Wave's tremendous popularity, the Bureau of Land Management had had to limit foot traffic to the area. This made the whole experience so much more enjoyable.

The four of us had hiked quite a few trails together, but most of those trails were marked—and well-worn. Getting to see The Wave involved a three-mile hike along this unmarked "trail" with a map and a compass. A few people in recent years have gotten lost on the way to The Wave and died from heat exhaustion. There were cairns to guide us along the way, and I certainly remembered a different set of cairns that saved my life when I was clawing my way out of the Syncline Valley. I was the lucky one then.

When we arrived, all the planning and wrangling to get permits were small prices to pay. What a sight to behold!

Water erosion created the Grand Canyon and many other canyons across our country. At The Wave, though, two main chutes were carved by water drainage that is long gone now. What remained were mounds of rock all around the chutes made out of windblown sand. Pink, yellow, and red Navajo sandstone stripes arced up, one over the other.

The four of us enjoyed camping together for a week. Years had passed since we had camped anywhere together, and we weren't as spry as we used to be. We weren't paddling on lakes anymore, stripping the blueberry bushes for pancakes in the morning. But we were good friends who had grown a great deal in our years apart. It was a testament to the bond formed, rather tenuously, when we were younger and more immature.

The Wave that washed over this desert area in the Southwest millions of years ago connected four old friends who had shared many excursions in the wild—four adults who had struggled in the intervening years and aged considerably. Pam and Henry provided two penetrating mirrors for Gene and me. We passed hours at our campsite reminiscing about the highlights of our outings together. I kept thinking that with no more water eroding the area, wind remains the main force that continually changes the landscape. For us it is age, yet each grain of sand holds the parts of us we still cherish.

But there was one low point. I had an apology to make.

There had been times on our outings together when we didn't all want to do the same thing. Even among the four of us, there could be unspoken competition about who had the most interesting sighting, or found the best campsite, or cooked the best meal for dinner.

On one trip, Pam and Henry had elected one day to stay at the campsite, though I wanted them to come with us to explore a tributary into Lake Argo. Gene and I took off without them, but I was feeling resentful.

Paddling along this narrow and rocky tributary, we came almost face to face with a giant, snapping turtle it took some maneuvering to get away from. We were momentarily terrified that we'd lose control of the canoe, spill into the water, scramble to get upright, and fail to retrieve all of our belongings. Fortunately, snapping turtles aren't aggressive and posed no danger to us. I wacked it lightly with my paddle, anyway, to get it out of our way. We continued on, breathing a heavy sigh of relief.

I couldn't wait to go back to our friends and talk about it. But it wasn't simply a fun thing to share. There was an angry edge to it, a "Ha, Ha, see what I found!" right out of second grade, petty, and intended to make them regret staying behind.

"Do you two remember the snapping turtle incident at Argo?" *Was I opening a pandora's box?* "At that point in my life, I guess I still enjoyed one-upping people."

"Oh, we all do sometimes. None of us is perfect."

Were they letting me off the hook?

"Well, thanks for the perspective. But I can't believe what an ass I could be sometimes."

Henry and Pam exchanged looks, and Pam got up and sat next to me.

"Marilea," she said, our eyes meeting. "Everyone can be an ass sometimes. That was years ago and it's already forgotten. When I think of what we've all been through in the past twenty years—between Gene's cancer and Henry's stroke—I'm happy that we're still fit enough to be doing trips like this. As to the snapping turtle incident, forget it. Water under the bridge," she insisted.

Interesting reference to water, as we sat there reminiscing in the desert.

Relationships can get crazy and complicated, like the desert swirls. But I was happy to unburden myself of feelings that had been weighing on me. Making amends is important in our lives, keeping the accumulation of guilt and resentments at bay.

There's a lot of freedom in that.

The Prius and The Babies

In our little, pueblo-style house between Albuquerque and Santa Fe, Gene had been happily involved in starting his fruit business, one peach tree at a time: Saturns, Challengers, China Pearls, Belles of Georgia. Ah, I can't forget the Rainier cherries, all those succulent apples, and even Shiro plums. He was in Heaven, the master of his own fruit utopia. Just as I was completing my project in Virginia, Gene was marveling at his flourishing orchard.

Gene's orchard in New Mexico.

Then, in the fall of 2009, Bridget moved there herself. She drove to Salt Lake City where Gene flew to meet her and help her drive back to Albuquerque. It was a long drive and they'd be together in her car for long periods. She wanted him to stop smoking, as did I, and he figured it was time. He couldn't fight us both. He quit smoking then, cold turkey, and has never returned to it.

Albuquerque has a vibrant community theater, and Gene and Bridget have always shared an appreciation of opera, theater, and all of the performing arts. They attended and participated in a number of theater performances, both separately and together, while Gene lived in New Mexico. They did Shakespeare, as well as modern theater. Gene was grateful for this closeness with his daughter, another reason why he was happy living there.

My son, Carter, had finished his master's degree in business in Austin, Texas, and he and his lady, Carrie, decided to get married. They had a picturesque and memorable "destination" wedding in the hill country outside of Austin, and all of the friends and family who could make their way to Texas celebrated their commitment to each other.

Annie was nearby, in Palm Springs, and in a rare and blissful period of sobriety. Her brother asked her to give a reading at the ceremony and her presence on that day made Carter's wedding nearly perfect.

Ten months after the wedding, I was still at school in Arlington when Carter called me in joyful tears that Quinn had been safely delivered on February 17. I can't describe the joy I felt at having become a grandmother for the first time. He and Carrie had since moved to Seattle, and I flew out there as soon as I could, the first of many trips to celebrate my grandchildren.

About a minute later it seemed, Carrie was pregnant again, and Emily Carter Rabasa arrived healthy and sound in August 2011. By then, I had moved to New Mexico, and Gene and I packed our Prius with an abundance of baby gifts and made our way up to Seattle. I couldn't wait to see Quinn and his baby sister.

While we were there, my son took Gene aside.

Putting an arm around Gene's waist, Carter said, "I'm so sorry that you've been going through cancer, Gene. Carrie and I were shocked to hear this news. I imagine it's been really scary, and we hope that you'll beat it. But I want you to know how much I appreciate your presence in Mom's life. I'm grateful for you."

The two men hugged each other. "Thank you, Carter. It means a lot to hear you say that."

Emily and Quinn, 2012.

My daughter, Caroline, had flown in from San Francisco, and we all "oohed" and "aahed" at baby Emily. She was a beauty with blue-blue eyes and a perky temperament. Carter and Carrie were exhausted, of course, trying to keep two babies happy.

"Is she a good baby, Carter? Does she sleep a lot?" we asked.

"Emily likes to be held." He smiled, his droopy eyes betraying his fatigue.

"Well, that's how babies are," we chirped. "Take heart. They grow up so fast."

In the course of just two years, Gene's and my world had gotten much bigger. And richer.

Those two babies were not unlike Gene's fruit orchard in New Mexico. We had entered a new phase of our lives, one rich with hope and longing, just as we had hopes for our own children. Now, a new generation was springing to life.

From our patio viewing the ruby sunset on Sandia Mountain, we felt the emotional pull tugging at us. I realized that our time in New Mexico had been a place to pause, a place to heal, a place to renew our hope for the future. It was not our final destination, but rather a critical milestone on our journey home.

So, we set about making a very complicated move to the West Coast. We wanted to be near those babies and watch them grow up.

Life, in all its renewal, goes on.

Tinkerbelle at the Market

I was selling the fruits of my garden in Rio Rancho at the Corrales Growers' Market one blisteringly hot, blindingly sunny day in August, nestled safely in a corner with maybe forty other sellers, slicing sample wedges off one of my fat, juicy, white Saturn peaches. To be modest, those peaches that summer were the finest ever grown in New Mexico. Okay, the world. Two years after I planted them, the trees had grown and produced abundantly. Marilea was with me now permanently, and she was as excited as I was to see and taste so many delicious peaches.

"Honey," Marilea complained, "I can't stand the heat right now. It's really slow here, anyway, so I'm gonna go back to the house. What on earth are we gonna do with all these peaches? Can you find someone to help you load up the crates and deliver them to churches?"

"Oh, ye of little faith! I have a feeling our luck is gonna change."

"If you say so, darlin'," Marilea said, kissing me before leaving the market. Sweet, juicy-yet-firm explosions of delicate peach essence. And there I stood in my small corner table setup, cutting bait, if you will, to lure customers. I had a bumper crop, too many to sell.

And, out of nowhere, from a blind spot of my little corner stall, a tiny, bent, black-clad, umbrella-toting old woman, looking mean and ornery, emerged. She was head-to-toe dressed in heavy dark wool on a stiflingly hot day and looked homicidal. Kill anybody, and you'll do.

Slowly, warily, and with measured pace, she scanned my two tables of summer crops displayed alongside the peaches. She pointed her umbrella at my white donuts, Saturns, the ones I took great pride in.

"What are *those?*" she snarled.

Well, ma'am," I started, "these are my Saturn peaches. Try a taste?" I proffered a fair chunk on the point of my Buck knife. Suspiciously, she grabbed the sample, popped it into her mouth, chewed and swallowed, and then turned into Tinkerbelle. She straightened up tall, broke into a broad grin, her eyes bright and smiling, and practically yelled, "My God, that's the best peach I have *ever* tasted!!!"

She bought two dozen and with great cheer passed among the crowd, giving away some of her purchase to little kids and pointing out my stand.

Marilea would have been delighted.

East to West in a Loaded Corolla with Old Tires in a Snowstorm

By 2014, those two babies had become toddlers. Gene and I were missing time with them, all the "firsts," like starting to walk and talk, that we could never get back.

Still staying for brief periods in the Virginia condo while I visited friends there, I was flying back and forth to Seattle regularly. But whether I was flying there from the east or from New Mexico, it wasn't the same as living where the kids were.

"Mom, when are you gonna get tired of throwing your money down the toilet?" my son asked me, exasperated. "Nobody else is living in your condo. You could be making a bundle renting it. Actually, just sell it and move up to Seattle to be closer to me, Carrie, and the kids." he pleaded.

I rarely traveled back east, now that I wasn't working there anymore. There seemed little reason to continue with all the up-keep and responsibilities. And I needed cash to help buy property in Washington State.

I felt so grateful that Carter wanted us nearby.

In February 2015, Gene and I did the hard work of preparing the condo for sale and packing up my belongings. There was a daunting amount of coordination required to have my household goods arrive in Washington State where I hadn't even yet bought a house.

For five years, my neighbor had been taking my blue Corolla out for a spin, just to keep the battery from dying. But those four tires . . . neither Gene nor I paid any attention to what should have been an obvious task: replace them before we undertook such a long drive out west. In February.

But we hadn't. As we crammed as much as we could into my little sedan, weighing it down and heavy to the gills, Gene and I said goodbye to our roots. And didn't look back.

Once again, we had pushed the envelope, this time taking a chance that my tires would survive the trip. Reckless? You bet. We still lived on the edge at times, tempting fate.

Deciding to take Route 40, the southern route across the country, we could see a couple of places we'd never been. Elvis Presley is one of Gene's all-time favorites, and Memphis was our first stop. We couldn't leave there without visiting the Gibson Museum. Gene's Gibson guitar is still one of his prized possessions.

We stopped in Oklahoma City to visit the Oklahoma Museum of Art and were completely bowled over by the Dale Chihuly exhibit of glassworks. I'd never seen anything like it. The sheer artistry of it all, the colors and creativity. This was glassblowing to perfection.

As we came out of the museum that afternoon, the city was hit with a blinding blizzard. We didn't dare stay in a motel overnight, afraid that we'd get snowed in. So we got back on the Interstate and prayed that the storm was moving east.

It wasn't. It remained with us, stalking us for nearly one hundred miles, all the way to Texas. I don't know how we managed to stay on the road with no snow tires. But it was slow-going. Most people were crawling along, except for the lunatic on a motorcycle bent on showing his captive audience how it should be done.

We eventually saw the wiped-out motorcycle and an ambulance five miles down the highway.

Somewhere in Texas, we found a motel and slept, waking up to dry roads and a sunny day. It was a straight shot from Texas back to Albuquerque.

A week after we got back, we had our first blowout, the right rear tire, a mile from the house. Two days later, the left rear went flat on our way to Santa Fe.

Afraid to get another flat, I took the Corolla into my tire place and discovered that all four of my tires were completely bald. When I thought of the snowstorm in Oklahoma and all the long stretches of highway far between towns, I looked up at the sky and thanked the Lord for sparing us that misfortune. The car was so tightly packed that we couldn't have even reached the spare without tossing everything onto the side of the road.

So . . . four new tires on the Corolla so that my daughter, Caroline, and her best friend could fly in and drive it back to San Francisco. Now that I was selling the condo, I didn't need a car in Virginia, so I offered to give it to her after Gene and I drove it to New Mexico. We are an economical family.

"Take my twenty-five-year-old car, Cal. Think of all the money I'm saving you!"

"Oh, yes, sure. I'd love it. Thanks, Mama! It will help me so much getting around to my jobs."

We'd arranged the logistics a few months earlier, and settled on a date for her arrival in Albuquerque. She and her friend had heard about the cachet of New Mexico and were thrilled to come for a visit, experiencing the Native American culture everywhere they looked. But a week of sightseeing and driving back to San Francisco was all the time they had off from work. And Caroline was happy to be retiring her bicycle to her back hallway.

My youngest child, "my flower child," I call her, or "Cal," left me and her whole family back in Virginia when she was eighteen years old. She needed space apart. Three thousand miles.

She had been depressed but participated in therapy first in Virginia and then in San Francisco. She went to Cal State East Bay and graduated five years later. Caroline has always done what she wanted to do. She's a free spirit and independent. And I'm proud of my daughter for the things that matter most to me: she has character, she's honest, she's hard-working, and she's empathetic and kind.

When she first moved to California, we wrote letters, she had some therapy, and we visited back and forth once or twice a year. She has dealt with the disappointments in her life, put things in perspective, and grown up on her own. These past twenty-two years, she's had different kinds of work, a few boyfriends, lots of friends, and good times. Over time, she's learned to trust me more, and we've become close. And she's always loved my handsome guy, Gene.

She, too, is estranged from Annie. They had been close growing up, and she grieved the loss of her sister for a long time. Twelve years ago, Cal got Crohn's disease, and I went to San Francisco to care for her while she was in the hospital. But she's learned how to manage it with new and improved drugs. She's busy with her own life now, trying to keep it as stress-free as possible. Out of necessity, she has detached from someone whose substance use disorder she has no control over. I wonder if she and Annie will ever reconnect. I still have hope.

I've made amends to many people in my life, but my children were at the top of the list. A few years ago, Caroline received my amends graciously and with kindness.

"Caroline, can you ever forgive me for obsessing over your sister during those early years of her illness? I guess it was easy for me since you were so far away. But that's a terrible excuse. And I'm sorry I neglected you when you were growing up. I mean, I know we can't go back and do things over, but I wish I'd made better choices when you needed me to be stronger."

"It's okay, Mama. I know you had a lot to deal with, and maybe we needed the time apart. I learned to grow up and take care of myself, and I think I'm stronger because of it. But I rely on you now more than anyone. And I appreciate the efforts you're making."

Caroline has grown into a lovely woman and she's happy with her life right now. That's enough for me. My job is to celebrate and love her—but always encourage independence.

When she first claimed hers in 2000, she drove east to west in a Mazda with her best friend, landing in San Francisco.

Fifteen years later, she would drive east to west, a bit more staid and in a Corolla this time, with another friend, but still landing in San Francisco.

Where Does the Sun Set?

At our beach on Camano Island.

A house by the sea was always a dream of mine—like returning to the womb. Scouting around in the Pacific Northwest, there were many properties to choose from. I looked at places where my own private beach was a stone's throw from my back door. Just gulp down my coffee, slip onto my beach, and into the surf for an invigorating wake-up call. But with the ice caps melting and beaches literally disappearing, I revisited my original dream and was grateful I had the good sense to be flexible and practical. Storms up here in the Puget Sound area can be violent, and these beaches bear little resemblance to the sleepy paradises I vacationed in when I was much younger.

So, I decided to go a bit higher, still with a beautiful view of the water and a bit of a walk down to my own private beach on Camano Island. But at least in my house on the hill I knew that the raging sea wouldn't be engulfing me in the middle of the night. And, Gene reminded me, tsunamis do happen here. But by the time the water gets up to us, we'll be on the roof launching our trusty Royalex canoe, helping out some frantic islanders hitching a ride.

In September 2015, Gene and I settled on the house by the sea we had hoped to find. He was thrilled about living on the water, feeling the sand between his toes, and smelling the salt air every day. Our new home brought back the best memories of our childhoods. We still had time to live out a few of our dreams.

To that end, we put our three canoes on top of Gene's and my cars, and caravanned the boats up to our new home. Now we could put our lonely, dusty old canoes to use. Saratoga Passage, part of the Salish Sea, would become our new playground.

Sometimes I imagine myself a boatwright
fashioning strong hulls to order for others.
I work with mature hardwoods and I love each
quirky knot and each stressed knurl as I love
the fine line of the grain, the strength,
the mute essence of beauty within.

I don't work from plans well,
so my customers know better than to provide
blueprints to follow. And they know
I don't keep well to schedules, being ill at ease
in shoal time.

Sometimes I wander off

But I do come back,
Lord willin' and the creek don't rise,
To my labors.
For love abides in and for the working
both of and toward what is lasting and true.

Perhaps we find ourselves at our best
Simply messing about in boats.

—Gene, Christmas Day 2015, on our beach at Camano Island

The Master Gardener

Our new home on Camano Island came with an already tilled garden ready for planting, and Gene has planted several trees here. We nourish the soil and hope for enough sunlight.

Gene also loves growing things from seeds. He finds the process fascinating.

Each year, he puts something different into the earth. We have so much kale that we've grown used to it in salads. And every year, he puts in tomatoes, daring them to last on the vine until Thanksgiving like they did in New Mexico. They never do. In our western Washington climate, produce grows at a vastly different rate than in sunnier climes.

But corn. Gene has been planting it ever since our first years together. In the plot he cut out of my green zoysia grass in Virginia, corn was a bust. In New Mexico, even with a soaker hose, it was a bust. But three's a charm. Last summer, we savored the most delicious corn on the cob we'd ever had—anywhere. Right out of our own garden. Twelve years after earning his gardener's credentials, he was living out one of his fondest dreams here on the island. And I, though reluctant at first in New Mexico, had grown to appreciate the challenge and satisfaction of growing things in the earth. Proficient weeding, for example, is very spiritual. It's like cleaning house, and it's a daily practice for me. I also enjoy pruning because it keeps the trees and plants tidy (and more fruitful). Best of all, I love sharing our bounty with friends and family.

There's a great deal of romanticism in farming. A farmer's success depends on elements of skill, timing, and the weather. When it works, his family eats. When weather destroys his crops, it doesn't. Fortunately for Gene, gardening is a pleasurable hobby and not a necessity for survival.

I've often wondered why Gene, the citified man who grew up and went to school in Cleveland Park, D.C., and Bethesda, Maryland, identifies so sincerely with farmers and all people who enjoy getting their hands dirty from working in the soil.

Farming nourishes dreams.

I know that as Gene and I slide into old age and lose so many loved ones, it's deeply gratifying to know that we do have power over some things. That even if a hailstorm hits and kills all the tomatoes, which happened in New Mexico, we can just plant some more. Next year.

So, though I'd never been interested in gardening, I loved Gene enough to keep an open mind about it. I've learned to appreciate time spent with my hands in the slug-filled dirt: planting seeds and removing weeds. It's really, I suppose, just a lesson in how we try to live our lives every day. The growing of things, nurturing and tugging some plants along, gives us satisfaction. It gives us a delicious sense of expectation.

Gardening keeps hope alive in us every year.

Tugging Plants Along

After we bought our house on Camano Island, I lived there by myself in the summer and Gene went to New Mexico to check on his orchard. He had friends there who helped him out.

It was important for me to stay on Camano, alone, if necessary, so that my

With the grandkids, 2015.

grandchildren could spend time with me there. This was valuable "grandma time" for us, taking them to the beach, doing lots of organized arts and crafts activities, storytelling and cooking together.

"Bela," Emily implored. "Let's make wheat bread today. I've watched Mom do it and it tastes *so* good. But we need wheat flour."

She looked into the baking cupboard.

"Do you have any?"

"No, we don't, you monkey," quick to hug her as I teased, "so I guess we'll have to go to IGA again. But I'm not buying you any more popsicles. We can make them ourselves at home."

I bought popsicles anyway.

Emily was only five when her parents started sending her to Camano Island. That was pretty young. I remember one night waking up to her whimpering on the sofa. I slept in the loft and it was just below me. I went right downstairs to hug her and reassure her. We sat together while I read *Grandmother's Stories*. When her eyes started closing, I closed the book and carried her up to our big, king-sized bed.

Playing checkers on San Juan Island.

The next day, I played the CD of *Grandmother's Stories*, read by Olympia Dukakis. All day long. She must have been so tired of it. I think I played it for myself.

Emily did get homesick sometimes, and when that happened, I was at a loss. I wanted to be the best grandma ever, and I think at times I fell short. It was times like that that I missed Gene and wished he'd been with me to help with the kids. He had such an easy way with them, telling jokes, and going about his business almost as though they weren't there. In other words, not trying too hard.

I did try too hard at first. Carter and Carrie were trusting me with their children, and I was afraid to make any mistakes. I coddled them too much, I think, and wasn't good at setting boundaries. But as I've grown in recovery, I've gotten better at that too. It's easier to say "no" now.

Quinn seemed to really enjoy himself on the island. One day, he helped me wash my car. And that young child rode his bicycle, with me on mine behind him, for a mile. We both had to walk our bicycles at the end, but what a trooper!

One summer, when Gene was visiting, he, Quinn and I went for a paddle in the Malecite.

"Quinn, look at that old tugboat washed up on the shore. I wonder if anyone lives in it."

"Yeah."

"Look how clean the water is, Quinn. You can see all the way to the bottom!"

"Yeah."

"You're awfully quiet, Lamb. What are you thinking about?"

What are the two most terrifying words to a grandparent? I'm bored.

"I'm bored."

"Oh." With an audible sigh, I turned to Gene, "What do you think, honey? Time to go back?"

"I'll turn around, but I want to go east beyond the jetty a little. The high tide often brings the whales up the Passage. Let's see if we can see any. Then we can go back."

Turning to my grandson, I asked, "Sound good, Quinn?"

"Yeah."

Then he smiled.

Water Ways

Not yet ready to let go of our resplendent view of the Sandia Mountains at sunset, Gene and I held on to the New Mexico property until we grew tired of hopping back and forth between two states as though it were a quick jaunt. As much as we basked in the warm, New Mexico sunshine, the excitement of the monsoons, and the incomparable sound of opera serenading the surrounding hills, the pull of water had been inevitable.

After we bought the house on Camano Island, fence-sitting became our hobby for the next four years. And we learned an important lesson: splitting our lives and activities between two towns greatly diluted the benefits of all of those activities.

Gene had planted a rose garden in New Mexico, putting in a rose for each of our five children. Then, on the trellis between the garden and the patio, he planted baby roses for the grandchildren. After five years, we realized how demanding roses were. They needed water, in addition to sunshine. By going back and forth from New Mexico to Puget Sound, we were away from the rose garden for long periods, and the blooms soon succumbed to our abandonment. We knew that we couldn't keep up with the maintenance any longer. After a decade, our days were numbered in the land of enchantment.

Neither of us had the back for all the work. We left the house under management in 2019 and returned to Camano Island permanently.

"It's been a grand adventure, honey," I said, hoping to cheer him up as he looked at his dying orchard. "You achieved a wonderful thing."

"Now, let it go," I continued. "Let's go live on an island with our boats and grow old together."

But even for me, a few things in the high desert have been hard to let go of. The monsoon sky in New Mexico was frightening and breathtaking, a magnificent red, pink, and yellow kaleidoscope hovering behind dark, eerily silent, ominous clouds. Desperate for the explosion of water, I stood outside with my arms open to welcome the downpour. My gratitude journal recorded every monsoon we experienced, nature playing its musical instruments: trombones for the thunder; trumpets for the outburst of rain from the dark clouds; violins serenading the countryside afterwards, soaking in the nourishment of water.

I would dearly miss looking up at the sky at an impending storm, the striking palette of colors, the air still and menacing as I prayed for a pounding downpour.

In wet western Washington, you won't find me doing that.

From my home on the west side of Camano Island, many mornings at dawn, the western horizon has bands of blue, then pinkish-orange rising like horizontal stripes over nearby Whidbey Island. At just the right time, the pink hovers over the Olympic Mountains, still jagged and dark, punctuating this band of color. Then I sit and watch the coloring fade as the sun in the east starts to come up over the island and change the light, muting the colors. As it rises in the sky, the sun will shine down on the Olympics, looming over Saratoga Passage and Whidbey, which parallels Camano; they look like ghosts in the snow-filled crevices with chocolate ice cream cones trickling down.

The Last Watch

My God, it's peaceful.

    Good Lord, it's still.

One elongated stretch of thin white cumuli
sits passive above the calm waters of Saratoga Passage
slowly shifting in sync with the soft surface breeze

I feel on my deck.

Stellar's Jays often land with a thud on the railing,
    but more often glide softly in for lunch at the feeder,
    as chickadees and wrens and swallows flit about . . .

After the forenoon slides past midday, the clouds thin out,
and the high, late May sun burns and blazes
through the endless blue above.

It is time to prep the garden . . .

—Gene, March 2022

Sky View

On Camano, I wake up sometimes on warm summer nights and go out onto my deck to look at the night sky. It barely rained at all last summer and the clarity in the heavens had been amazing. There is very little light pollution here on Puget Sound. But on one particular night, I was in for a visual delight that I had never had and probably would not have again.

"Make it zebra-like," I always tell my hairdresser. "It's so boring if it's all the same color. Put streaks of white here and there to blend in with my white sides. But weave it in and out with what's left of the dark."

In similar fashion, this night sky had bands of shimmering white stars, all in different widths, stretching from horizon to horizon, with the darkness of space, like my brown hair, providing the contrast to appreciate this glimmering show. When I first saw this display as I sleepily sauntered onto the deck, I couldn't quite believe it. I did a double- and then a triple-take.

In my excitement, I went upstairs and woke Gene out of a sound sleep.

"Honey, come outside and look at the sky. I think I'm looking at the Milky Way!"

Shuffling onto the deck, he carefully observed the sky and the glittering spectacle of stars. Then he corrected me. "No, I don't think so. But it sure is pretty, Toots, jus' like you," he joked, squeezing me from behind. "Come back to bed."

With further research, I learned that the Milky Way was very different from what I saw. I don't know what it was I saw, but it was striking, anyway.

I've been fortunate to see a natural phenomenon—I'll call it "My Milky Way"—to remember how small I am in the scheme of things. How my life and problems are absolutely insignificant when viewed next to larger, more important things that have pressing consequences for the world and its population. It lifts me out of the mire of my own ego and brings me closer to the peace and serenity I seek. And I need to be reminded of this on a regular basis.

Humbling.

Mirrors

When I moved to New Mexico in 2010, the first thing I did was join Gene as a substitute teacher in Rio Rancho Public Schools. We got up at the crack of dawn every day for about seven years. I'd missed being in a classroom, and the paychecks came in handy.

I threw the rest of my energy into finding some semblance of peace in my life, though even that—quieting the self-destructive forces holding me down—would take a few more years. I continued to work at my twelve-step recovery programs that I had begun in Virginia in 2002, going to a meeting a day. A stubborn, slow learner, it was nevertheless critical for me to continue reevaluating myself and my life. There were many things I needed to change to be happy and at peace. But I wasn't there yet. I was still drinking.

The daily meetings of several twelve-step groups forced me to look honestly in the mirror and choose: did I want to keep hiding from my fears behind my illness; or did I want to learn how to live well? I had resolved to stop using food as a weapon to hurt myself, and it had a positive effect on the eating disorders I'd struggled with since I was a teenager. I stopped purging altogether. I remember the day I told Gene about this compulsion I'd had for so long.

"Honey, I'm sure you've noticed when I've occasionally pigged out over the years. Most people do, but I always followed it by throwing up afterwards. I never told you about it. I was so ashamed, and such a coward to have kept it from you. I never want to keep secrets from you."

"Are you still purging?"

"No. Look, I know you love me, and I need to know you love all of me."

"I always have." I heard the disappointment in his voice. "I'm sorry you didn't know that." Then he looked me in the eye and took my hand. "Babe, I've always loved and accepted you, even your dark side. Who am I to judge you as flawed as I am?"

We hugged. Gene had to leave for the farmer's market. But I felt quite a bit lighter.

Trust. Oh, yes. I still had a ways to go . . .

Then I started publishing books and essays, a powerful factor, it turned out, in my healing work. Writing down my thoughts and feelings was like spelunking in a cave. It was in that darkness that I discovered hidden truths about myself and my early life with my family. Those discoveries enlighten me to this day.

According to the Greek legend, Narcissus fell in love with his own reflection in a pool. The modern term "narcissist" has come to mean anyone who loves himself to distraction, often sacrificing the well-being of others.

I am not like Narcissus. When I was younger, walking along any street where there were stores, if I saw my reflection in the windows, I turned away. With critical eyes, healthy self-esteem has been a struggle for me.

Most of my life has been a wrestling match between the good wolf and the bad one. In many ways, the good wolf won: I'd always been an enthusiastic volunteer; I followed through with college and grad school; I worked hard to be a good teacher; and I wanted to be the best parent/grandparent I could be. But from a young age, my inner critic often sabotaged my efforts. I was so insecure that any fault seemed unforgiveable. And I turned to substance use as a coping mechanism: first food, then amphetamines, and finally alcohol. I was feeding the bad wolf for years. I stopped abusing amphetamines many years ago, and then, over time, eating became nothing more than a necessary way to nourish my body. But, up until five years ago, I drank to get drunk. And the drinking incidents were increasing.

Now that Gene and I were living close to my son and grandchildren, I was spending a great deal of time at Carter's in Seattle. I drank in his basement, secretly quaffing all of his vodka. What was I thinking? That he wouldn't notice the empty bottles? He did notice, and wasted no time staging an intervention with me. Carter and Carrie asked me to come down to Seattle. This was my final unmasking.

"Why aren't you two at work today?" I asked them. It was a weekday and I wondered why they were home.

"This is more important, Mom. Come, sit down. We need to talk."

Uh, oh, I felt myself cringing. *I know that tone of voice so well. The one from my French professor who noticed parts of my term paper sounded a lot like the blurb on the jacket of a novel. Another shortcut.*

My fear was growing.

"Mom, we know you've been drinking vodka from our supply behind the bar downstairs. The bottles are nearly empty, and no one else here drinks vodka."

Naked . . . naked . . . naked. I felt like I'd been skinned alive, with everything beneath the surface exposed, scenes from *Predator* making me nauseous. There was nothing I could do. I felt so ugly.

"Mom, what is going on with you? Is it Annie? Why do you need to drink secretly like that? Why don't you drink upstairs with us? No big deal. It's not the drinking that bothers us; it's the secrecy."

Next, the avalanche of tears: the divorce, the angry and depressed children. Carter and Carrie rushed to my side, supporting me, compassionate.

I hung my head in shame. What a dreadful and mortifying experience. Humbling.

And, ultimately, edifying.

It was the giant mirror we all fear but at the same time require if we want to be our best in the world.

That did it for me. When I saw the look in their eyes, the worry, distrust, and fear, that was suddenly too high a price to pay for the numbness I got from guzzling large amounts of vodka.

That is the bottom many substance users need to reach before they're willing to stop. And once again, my guardian angel was with me. My bottom might have killed me—in a car or on a flight of stairs. Or I might not have been alone.

Children, I'm so sorry.

They didn't ask me to stop drinking. That was my decision. I wrote them a letter of amends a week later and hoped they would trust me again in time, these two loving and hopeful mirrors that told me I could transcend my limitations, that I could embody God's gifts.

I've learned a hard lesson over the years, that the only life I can save is my own. Surrendering my substance use and working on my emotional sobriety continues to ensure a better life for myself. My dear son and daughter-in-law nevertheless played an important role to that end. There's a poignant bond between us now. Though we rarely speak of it—the tamed elephant in the living room—it's there, an invisible thread, quite apart from our family connection. There's an intimacy between us that was never there before.

When my shortcomings had weighed me down for so many years, my son, through the power of his own forgiveness, has given me the chance to change. There's a lightness in my steps now, as I enjoy my grandchildren, and when I tell this story at meetings, sometimes with tears flowing around me, my heart is full.

I am one lucky lady. And mirrors? Bring them on.

A Spiritual Union

Back in the winter of 1996, the year Gene lived with me and the kids in Virginia, a mammoth snowstorm closed the schools for two weeks. Paid vacation for both of us! The blizzard ended quickly, but northern Virginia was blanketed in snow for a long time. Because of the rarity of big blizzards there, snowplows were in short supply.

What fun we had. Caroline and her friends went out to the woodpile so we could have fires all day long. Gene had to keep cutting more wood. We roasted marshmallows and made s'mores.

Gene and I bought cross-country skis at REI and skied all over McLean, enjoying the exercise of walking on skis. Aerobic, yes, but not exciting like some other sports. Not toned or athletic, I happily settled for healthy.

We were never bored with all the snow around us. It seemed like the mountains had come to us, and we skied wherever we could without getting hit by a car. Annie and Caroline were working at the bagel factory in one of the strip malls and we went to see them there. Skiing around was so much of a delight that we determined to keep it up as we got older. It was an energizing and healthy respite from our often-sedentary lives.

During those two weeks, Gene and I piled our cross-country skis on top of my Corolla sedan and headed for an area called Limberlost in the Shenandoah Mountains. It was there where we first began hiking with Henry and Pam, an easy, seventy-mile drive for us from northern Virginia. This trail was an undemanding loop that circled for about a mile, unlike many of the hiking opportunities that shot off the main roads like arteries. But though the trail was mostly flat, we climbed in the car to three thousand feet along Skyline Drive to reach it.

On those weekdays, we immediately felt the peace and quiet in the wooded hollows. I recognized the mountain laurel from my hike up Old Rag, and the tall oak trees seemed to hover over us, along with the towering hemlocks, creating a green umbrella along the path. In twenty-five years, these unlogged hemlock trees would be decimated by hemlock woolly adelgids, tiny, aphid-like insects. At the time, though, the wooded hollows became an excellent place for us to practice our cross-country skiing every winter, unlike the nearly impassable streets of northern Virginia after a storm.

"Gene, please, this is not a cross-country trail. Can't you see all the hills ahead of us? Up and down . . . up and down . . . all I can do is snowplow."

"Well, the book said this is one of the best cross-country trails up here. C'mon. We probably just have to find it from here."

"Sure, if I don't break my hip before I get there." Gene and I used to go skating at the sculpture garden on the Mall in Washington, D.C. In those days, I drank a four-pack of Cabernet just to get the courage to go onto the ice. If I fell down and broke my hip, as a friend of his had done, maybe it wouldn't hurt so much. Gene saw me guzzling the little bottles, but he knew better than to interfere. Fear ruled me then, and for many years afterwards.

"Babe, how 'bout we not worry about falling and just practice our skiing?"

Gene and I hadn't been together very long by 1996, but he was fast learning how to manage me and my crippling fears. We all have fears, but substance users seek relief from them with food, pills, or alcohol, to name a few. Even gambling, sex, or work are behaviors, when used to avoid problems and pain, that can become habitual. And substance use disorder, by definition, has the power to take over our lives. Fears either paralyze me into inaction or push me into actions that I might regret later.

Gene knew all about the addictive power of alcohol and how it temporarily numbed his pain. But reaching for a drink (or a brownie, or an illicit affair, or a snort of cocaine) was only a symptom of deeper problems. Through his recovery work, long before I ever met him, he had wrestled with his own demons, and found a solution that has kept him sober for thirty-six years. In twelve-step recovery programs, a big part of that solution is found in faith in something or someone outside of ourselves—be it God, or a tree, or the fellowship. He is devoted to his meetings and attends one or more nearly every day.

It would take me many years to let go of my fears and put my trust in something or someone else. Gene nurtured this spiritual growth in me the way he would later nurture his orchard.

"Love is a force. It is not a result; it is a cause. It is not a product; it produces. It is a power, like money, or steam, or electricity. It is valueless unless you can give something else by means of it."
—Ann Morrow Lindbergh

Of all the loves Gene and I have shared in our years together—from boats to opera to rock music to nature—it is our love of each other and those around us that has inspired me to grow with him as a sober adult, clear-eyed and stronger in my faith.

"Marilea, where is the *Daily Reader?* Let's do the reading for today," Gene said as he started every day with me. This reading was followed by jointly praying about any daily concerns we might have. This form of togetherness has strengthened our bond as we've grown in recovery. Just as I've changed over the years, so has he. But the thread of faith has been a grounding force in our relationship as we've grown older.

When Annie was in trouble, my instinct was to rescue and protect her from harmful consequences. It was losing my child to the torture of substance use disorder that led me, quite accidentally, into confronting myself and the landscape of my own inner conflict. And in so doing, ironically, it was I who came away more healed, less broken, and more able to accept—with grace—the disappointments in my life. Now, after years of recovery, I know that those same consequences might have been her best teachers. This is precisely where faith might have helped me; I didn't have any when I most needed it.

It's been a slow wheel, my road to recovery. Gene and my friends in recovery have been a constant guide in the art of living well. My love for him and the rest of my family has broken down my stubborn resistance and given me hope for a happier, more productive life.

"The resistance to praying is like the resistance of tightly clenched fists. This image shows a tension, a desire to cling tightly to yourself, a greediness which betrays fear."
—Henri Nouwen

A home in the woods was my childhood sanctuary. In those woods, I was in charge; I set the stage for happy interactions between my family members and me. But the world outside of my fantasies was harsh and unforgiving. I did not have the tools then to grapple with my disappointment and sadness. So I stumbled and floundered. Though I appeared to be doing all the right things later on—I went to college, married, had children, and even enjoyed a fulfilling career in teaching—on the inside, I was lost and as thirsty as the desert in New Mexico.

Guided by the principles in my twelve-step programs, my increasing ability to love, first myself and then those around me, has been the one constant on this spiritual journey. Letting go of guilt and blame and accepting accountability for my choices has helped me mature. Despite the difficulties I've faced, staying on that positive path has opened the door to a peace and contentment that I'd never known before.

I've found my safe place, and it's within me.

Part Five:
COMING HOME

"The best journey takes you home."
—Author unknown

Now

He has great affection for my grandchildren: Quinn, now twelve, and Emily, who just turned eleven. They call him Grampy Gene, but some days, if he doesn't get enough sleep, he's Grumpy Gene. No matter, he loves them anyway, and I think they're growing fond of him too. He would enjoy teaching them more about boats and musical instruments.

Jamming with Quinn.

When we first moved up to Camano, we wanted to share some of our interests with the children, and ice skating was on the list. There's an indoor rink near us at Shoreline. One day, Carter and Carrie brought the kids to meet us there and they rented skates for them. My son knew this would be another happy memory that

I was racking up in my golden years. I had been emotionally absent during much of his childhood, and he was generously offering me a second chance with his children. I didn't want to miss any opportunities.

Quinn, brave as ever, rushed onto the ice for the first time, fell down, and got back up. He did this many times, grimly counting his spills. He would remember the number and determine to fall down less when we took him again. Competitive? Yes. Proud? Sure! A motivator.

Emily was shy on the ice and clung to the sides, but relaxed if I held her hand. We went around quite a few times and Gene took her out as well. But she tired of it and went to the snack bar for hot chocolate.

Gramps was doing great. He's a good skater, back on the ice after a few years. He was just getting his "ice legs," skating backward and doing leg lifts on one skate, moving slowly to keep his eyes on Quinn. But moving too slowly was a mistake.

Oops! He's not so young anymore. Splat! Right on all fours on the ice.

"No, no, I'm okay. I'll just get some ice," he insisted. But later, as we were leaving, he whispered, "Marilea, will you drive? My wrist hurts."

Next day, X-rays at Urgent Care, double wrist fracture, Ibuprofen.

"Geez, Marilea! We shouldn't have told the kids. Now they'll feel guilty we took them skating."

"No, they won't. They'll be grateful for our shared experience."

That's how I feel these days: grateful for twenty-nine years of experiences with Gene. His affection for my grandchildren springs from his love for me. He has grown to care about my children in the same way. It can be like that in loving relationships, but I know plenty of blended families who have a devil of a time getting along. Gene has always tried to step up and grow to love those closest to me: my friends, family, and now my grandchildren. And I have reciprocated with his family. Gene's children and siblings are an extension of him, and they know that they hold a firm place in my heart.

Bridget and Patrick have visited us on Camano Island. On one of those visits a few years ago, Bridget and I were strolling on our beach. I stopped walking, picked up another shell for my collection, then tossed it back where it belonged.

I turned to look at her. "I need to make an amends to you, Bridget."

She turned to look at me, curious.

"Early on, all those years when we still lived in Virginia, I didn't try to get to know you much. I don't think we ever had any one-on-one time together, taking you to lunch, or just a cup of tea, so we could talk and get to know each other better. You've always been close to your father, for which I am grateful. But I could have tried harder to build a relationship with you. I'm sorry about that. Definitely my loss."

Looking surprised to hear these words pour out of my mouth, she offered, "Oh, thanks for saying that! You know, I could have tried harder too."

"Well, it's never too late to try and do better."

We continued our walk, chatting. But I was relieved to clear out a little more of the "clutter of remorse," as I call it, that had been weighing on me. I'm very fond of Bridget.

Gene's not the same man now that he was when we fell in love in 1993. He's still tall and bends a bit at the shoulders to stay on eye level with people. But he has terrible arthritic pain in his back and hands. Eschewing painkillers, he wears a back brace and soldiers through the days. His head of blonde, curly hair has gone mostly white, but his eyes are still icy blue. He still pays attention to me in all the sexy ways, and never leaves the house without a kiss and an "I love you!"

Some days—when I'm struggling and he can't make me smile—he might feel small and inadequate. Aware of this mood shift, I can't let him take responsibility for "fixing" me. I approach him from behind while he's seated, wrap my arms around his neck and tell him he's my knight in shining armor.

"I'm still your Toots, babe. I still adore you."

And I mean it.

I know how lucky I am to have spent my middle and golden years with this good man. Every day when I wake up, I look at him hard. I feel his presence in my life, not his body, but his spirit and joy—and I say, "Thank you, Lord." Maybe we won't be together next year or in five years. Maybe one of us will pass on and the other will be left to feel the void. But I'm so grateful for the comfortable partnership I have with Gene now.

It has not always been a happy journey, but how many relationships are constantly blissful? We stuck out the hard times, because we knew that life was better for us together than apart. We hoped that, like many puzzles that lose their pieces, we could find the missing ones and fit them together in the years we had left. One of those missing pieces was my spotty relationship with faith. It helped a great deal that I chose to get sober in 2017. That was the year this student was at last ready for the teacher.

In so many fundamental ways, Gene and I have been right for each other: our love of nature, boats, opera and all kinds of music, teaching and writing. But he has also carefully tutored me through my early recovery from alcoholism. Lately, we have shared our recovery on an international scope.

"Babe, I got the passwords to a recovery meeting on Zoom in Ukraine on Wednesday mornings. Let's make a point of attending, okay? It'll be nine o'clock our time," he pointed out.

"Great idea. I'll pass on the information at my meeting."

Long before I stopped drinking, he kept loving me in spite of my drinking bouts. He braved my slurred rants and verbal sparring; and he forgave me over and over again for being a much earlier version of himself. All he could do was pray that I would find enlightenment before I killed myself. And be there, with an open heart and a bushel of hope, to pick me up if I fell down.

Our relationship is more peaceful now as I'm learning to let go of my fears and rely more on faith. He has been my loyal partner all these years, even when I was drinking. Who knows how the stress of living with me has affected him?

Living with Others

Drunk or sober, life can impose stark choices—
 What defines the spirit, the essence
 Of recovery?

Gratitude first.

But the alcoholic always lives with tension—
 Do I choose a sober life for me
 Or is my past my future?

In every other sick-program friend
 I see myself reflected,
 Pray I might be of help—me, the helpless one—
 And I smirk and throttle a belly laugh
 And remember I must help myself first.

So I choose to stay in the present
 Sober/today

And pray my condition is contagious.

These days I get up with gratitude in my heart and work to stay emotionally sober. Free of the numbing haze of alcohol, I'm more clear-eyed. I still live with the same disappointments and pain that I always have, but years of recovery have offered me healthier perspectives on it. The key to this healthier perspective, I believe, is in acceptance. Reinhold Niebuhr's Serenity Prayer: "God grant me the serenity to accept the things I cannot change, the courage to change the things I can, and the wisdom to know the difference" is a well-known and highly useful philosophy. I cannot change the life Annie is living. She chose to walk away from her family ten years ago, and those years are lost. But I can choose to embrace all the blessings in my life and stay focused on what I can control. Gene sees my joy, he appreciates my gratitude, and he continues to cradle my grief around losing Annie in his loving arms. This lifts me up. He's free from tolerating my drunken binges or worrying about my driving. We alcoholics are a selfish lot when we drink, oblivious to its effects on our loved ones.

"I have five years this month, Carter," I tell my son on the phone. "Life is good."

"It's better than good, Mom," he responds. "You moving up here with Gene has made all the difference to me, Carrie, and the kids. And yes, I'm glad you've found a way to be happy without drinking. Congratulations!"

Yes, life is good.

Freedom

When I met Gene, I opened my mind to many new things. And one of them was learning more about all aspects of natural landscapes and the creatures that inhabited them. Birds, especially, fascinate Gene.

I spent my first thirteen years in a rural town in Massachusetts where the Thornton family was in charge of the local Audubon Society up in the woods on the western fringe of town. People from all around the Boston area came to study and celebrate nature. My parents took me there, and I remember the exhibition of stuffed birds in one of the rooms. But I wasn't always as curious as I might have been. Fearful and shut down, I was afraid to ask too many questions.

Nowadays, we sit on our deck feeding the finches and the greedy Stellar's Jays. The latter are so territorial and nasty. Well, if you were a little brown wren, wouldn't you be intimidated by the size of those blue feathers?

Squirrels can be pests, and watching another gray rodent hop onto our bird feeder, Gene dropped what he was doing, grabbed his slingshot and a couple of rocks. In a flash, he was on the deck giving it his best shot. His attack just scared away the squirrel, but we knew we had to get some squirrel-proof feeders.

Delighted now to be feeding our birds and not the squirrels every day, we are soaking in the array of birds we have, one of Camano Island's signature attractions. But boy, are they messy! When we first invested in all that birdseed to fill the feeders, we were just excited to see them appear in all their colorful glory. But a day didn't go by without my needing to sweep their refuse off the deck.

"Refuse" is an appropriate word: they refuse to eat the whole seed that we feed them. As they say at our recovery meetings, they took what they liked and left the rest. All over my deck. We finally learned to hang the feeders over the lawn as we imagine the rabbits and the squirrels fighting over the birds' refuse down below.

Gene strains his neck with his new binoculars, determining if it's an eagle or a hawk overhead moving into one of our tall evergreens. We wish one of those big raptors would build a nest that we could study from afar. He spends hours with his Peterson's bird book learning about birds.

I think he just wishes he could fly.

When Man (or Woman) Collides with Nature

Our maiden excursion with the Malecite on Saratoga Passage was memorable. Paddling one afternoon, Gene and I shushed each other and momentarily took our paddles out of the water. There, sunning itself on a protruding rock as the tide was receding, was a large seal, nonplussed by our approach.

Quietly, we advanced.

"Gene, paddle softly," I whispered. "Maybe we can get close enough for a picture."

"Okay. I'll circle the rock but give him a wide berth."

We were ten feet away and snapped a picture before the seal slid into the water and swam away, nose in the air, and miffed at our intrusion.

"Well, now that the seal is gone, make some noise with your paddle to startle the eagles, if there are any, out of the trees. I think I saw one up there," I turned to point out the top of a burned-out pine tree. Like a beaver signaling distress, Gene loudly slapped his paddle on the water.

It worked. One beauty took off high and majestic, showing off his eight-foot wingspan, in search of a more peaceful perch.

I still wince at a close encounter, a tragic one, I had a few years ago as I was driving north to leave the island. My car actually crossed paths with one of these beauties.

This particular fellow had the bad luck to hop out of the roadside bushes and choose that moment to fly low across the street to the other side. Only he didn't make it. I know birds have unmatchable eyesight; they wouldn't eat well if they didn't. But don't they have ears? Didn't he hear my car coming down the road?

Splat!!! Right into the front grill of my white car, bouncing back onto the road. *Did that really just happen?* I felt terrible as my heart did a leap into my throat. I realize now that he must have been injured to fly into a moving vehicle, but I was still stunned by what had just occurred.

Nervously checking the back seat, I had to keep driving, because I had my grandson with me and he was in a hurry to get home to Seattle. Can you blame him? His Bela—the eagle killer. He would have been heartbroken to see firsthand the fragility of our wildlife. And I couldn't bear to show him what human beings and their machines were capable of.

Fortunately, the eagle population has rebounded from near extinction. But not so many years ago, they were an endangered species. Now I had this to add to my list of accomplishments. Not proud of this at all.

I can still see him, a graceful, horizontal projectile—white-headed and white-tailed—as he began a low ascent that ended on the grill of my car. A beautiful bird, and one of several we had frequently seen while paddling along the shore of Saratoga Passage. Gene always splashed his paddle into the water to startle them enough to take flight. And what a sight it was when they did.

I felt doubly bad, because I didn't stop to move the bird's body to the side of the road. I knew other islanders would take care of this precious bird. But on my way home later that day, I honestly feared there would be a roadblock in the area, checking the grill on every passing car. Mine was smashed in with some telltale blood and feathers, and I was sure I'd be arrested for "reckless something or other."

Well, much to my relief, there was no roadblock, and I hastened up my driveway to scrub away the evidence from the broken grill—like a guilty criminal covering her tracks. Not daring to open my mouth and share my story with anyone, lest I become a pariah in my new neighborhood. I was certain there would be a story in *Camano Connections* the following month: "Speeding Car Kills One of Our Few Bald Eagles." Or worse: "Hit and Run Driver Sought for Careless Murder of Bald Eagle." My imagination was, of course, working overtime.

There was no story in the local paper, and at first no one noticed the broken grill on my car. When my son noticed it a few months later and asked me about it, I scrunched my eyebrows together, feigning puzzlement and lied, "Gee, someone must have backed into me in a parking lot. Don't you just hate people sometimes?" I held onto that lie for a couple of years until he asked me again how the grill had gotten smashed. This time I couldn't lie to him. Gene and I were visiting his family in Seattle.

"Carter, I can't lie to you anymore. My recovery is based on honesty, and it's not okay for me to cover up what I do. But here it is, the real story: an eagle, possibly sick and injured to use such bad judgment, flew low to the other side of the road just as I was coming toward him at forty-five miles an hour. He smashed right into the grill and flopped back to the side of the road. I couldn't stop just then, because it would have upset Quinn a great deal to witness the incident. So I just kept driving and got through the day. But I was mortified and ashamed, as though it were my fault."

"Oh, Mom, you should have said something! I know it wasn't your fault. I'm sorry you felt you had to lie about it."

"That's what many alcoholics do, Carter. It's our default setting. But I'm trying to change what used to come naturally to me. Please be patient with me."

Gene piped in: "Babe, you're too hard on yourself. Always have been. This was not your fault," he said, smiling as he changed the subject.

All kinds of wildlife are still in need of protection, and both Gene and I donate some of our money every year to that cause. But I was sad to have a crass modern invention like my RAV4 cross paths with one of nature's most beautiful birds—and unwittingly be a party to its destruction. Now, I am ever more mindful of the public's need to protect our wildlife and the wilderness that supports it, before it disappears into memory.

My grandchildren are growing up surrounded by nature, and that awareness will stay with them. My son is making sure to nurture their awareness with camping and hiking trips—all the joys of nature that he missed growing up. Knowing what futurists tell us is coming down the road, I cannot ask for more in this lifetime.

I Forgive—I Am Forgiven

"Dadsey" was my pet name for my father. He was a gifted but troubled man who missed his own father's attentions, my grandfather having spent much of his time living at the Harvard Club. I don't know when Dad began drinking. In 1935, being a drunk was sometimes romanticized. It was about that time that a few other alcoholics in Ohio decided to offer a spiritual means to managing alcoholism, and twelve-step recovery has been successful worldwide ever since.

Though Dad never tried that approach to recovery, he did try to give up drinking on several occasions. He loved my mother a great deal and no doubt was trying to please her. She was relentless in trying to get him to stop. But her nagging only alienated him, and their marriage in later years was hard to look at.

I had to look at it because I was the youngest child, and by the time my father was in his mid-fifties, he was on a roll with gin and looking for company.

"Look what I bought you at the corner store," he said as he gleefully pulled the grape wine out of the paper bag.

"No thanks," I told him, and I saw the disappointment in his eyes. I was just a teenager but not interested. I was into food then, not alcohol.

Like my father, Gene drank heavily while he was raising his children. Flawed, yes. But they were both good men without an ounce of malice in them. Troubled? Of course. But good men who loved their families unconditionally.

Also, like Gene, my father was a talented wordsmith. Starting around 1965, he wrote an annual Christmas poem until the year he died. Twenty years of Christmas poems were a lasting gift he gave our family. In this, his last poem, his love of family shines bright:

"Terraces" Revisited

This gathering here in '84 may not seem quite like those before.
Our children's children grow so fast,
But memories bring back the past.
There's still one-third, we're sorry to say,
Who couldn't make it here today.
Yes, Angel and his Marilea will share another Christmas tree
With Carter, Annalise, and Caroline too—all of them send their love to you.

His poem goes on to celebrate the accomplishments of his remaining six grandchildren in great detail. It's clear from all his poems over the years that his children and grandchildren were of paramount importance to him and my mother. He concludes the poem with news of him and his "bride," as he often called her:

You've heard our '84 report—now let your bard digress.
For Mother and for me there was indeed some happiness.
Harvard said, "Come back, you've been away for fifty years."
We had numerous occasions to fill the cup that cheers.
Then Mother's trip to England, and a bit of Scotland, too.
And Father's high school 55th—so many friends I knew.
It seems the year has quickly passed—a new one will unfold.
Our fiftieth year in '85 we'll celebrate in gold.
Each one of you, in your own way, has given us joy and pride.
Our love goes out to all of you—it reaches far and wide.

Dad died in September '85, three months before my parents fiftieth anniversary. They never celebrated that milestone.

If I was ever angry with my dad, that anger has folded itself into an understanding and love that can only be felt by another recovering alcoholic. All I would have to do was look at his twenty years of poems to see the goodness of heart in this man.

I, too, write a poem for each of my grandchildren on their birthdays to celebrate their lives. How lovely that, despite his flaws, Dad never failed to salute his children and grandchildren. He was a role model for me in some enduring ways.

My father, Gene, and I are kindred souls. And that kinship softens my edges and tempers the memories that might have embittered me, had I not found recovery. Dad adored us all, just as Gene and I love our own children. We did the best we could with who we were.

It's all so clear to me now.

Looking Back to See Ahead

"To look backward for a while is to refresh the eye,
to restore it, and to render it the more fit for its
prime function of looking forward."
—Margaret Fairless Barber

For twenty-four years, Gene had been my guide to many of the national parks in the United States and Canada. It was my turn, then, to be his guide. Angel and I had lived in Greece for three years and we saw many places, Crete being one of our favorite getaways in the summer. And in the winter, we occasionally went skiing with the children on Mount Parnassus near our house north of Athens.

I had promised Eleni, my close friend there, that I would come back to Greece three times before I died. So in 2017, I saw Greece that third and last time not only from a new and happier perspective, but in a different way.

With Gene, I wanted to see Greece differently. I wanted it to be our trip, an unforgettable one. So I took him to places I hadn't yet seen: a sea tour of Santorini, including the volcanic national park that included a challenging hike up to Manolas on Thirasía; and, an in-depth exploration of the Pelion Peninsula in northern Greece.

In addition to being Gene's guide and showing him the country, on this trip I was on a mission: not only to fulfill a promise to an old friend, but to find a way to let go of something holding me hostage. I was looking for redemption for choosing to divorce Angel and break up my family.

"So what's redemption got to do with it, babe?"

"Gene, c'mon! You know about the end of my marriage. Greece in the late '80s was where my life as I knew it went to hell, and I took Angel and the kids with me. I was beyond selfish. I had a full knapsack from the early years of my life and I just dumped it on the ground. Old stuff. Unresolved stuff. I needed to go back to the place where I determined to change my life, regardless of the cost."

"I know. I know. Stop feeling guilty about divorcing Angel. He bore much of the responsibility himself, you know. Don't forget that," Gene asserted.

Perhaps coming from his own experience, he knew all too well that it took two to make a marriage—and two to end it. Gene wanted to bring my focus back to the present. Perusing one of our guidebooks, he was determined to eat up the sights of local geology and many other rock formations in Greece. Fortunately, Greece had plenty of rocks.

One of those rocks was the island of Santorini in the Cyclades, famously written about in the Ulysses fables. I'd been there once or twice with Angel, and thirty years later, it's still a living museum of a volcanic eruption. Santorini and a few small islands are what remains of this eruption 3,500 years ago in that area of the Mediterranean Sea. We decided to focus our tour on a boat expedition down in the volcanic crater, a place Angel and I had missed exploring.

"Make sure to meet us back here in two hours. The entrance to the Santorini Volcano is just up ahead, and you need to buy a ticket," the tour guide warned us as we were disembarking on Nea Kameni, one of two uninhabited volcanic islands in the Santorini crater.

Strolling along the well-worn tourist route on this small island, I was disappointed by the lack of fire and drama I had seen at other volcanic sites around the world. But the views of the main island of Santorini were breathtaking—so breathtaking, I suppose, that Gene wasn't paying close attention to anything else.

"Gene, how many times do I have to ask you for our water bottle?" I hollered as he walked ahead of me. Exasperated and out of patience, I caught up with him to get a drink.

"Gee, thanks, babe. I'm really thirsty."

"Sorry, I didn't hear you."

"Why not? Are you wearing your hearing aids?"

Gene quickly checked them both, and I saw the alarmed look in his eyes as he frantically scanned the immediate path we had been walking on.

"Jesus, my left one is missing!"

"Oh hell, all we can do is retrace our steps and look for it."

"Yeah, look at the path where twenty-five other tourists have ground it into the dirt," he replied, borrowing my role as the fearful pessimist.

Hearing aids are ridiculously expensive and not covered by Medicare, so we did go over where we had been. For a while. We had some hope that another tourist would see us staring at the ground on the path and ask us if we had lost a hearing aid. No luck, though.

We were losing our focus. And we would miss the boat as it was leaving.

Oh, well . . . they're insured.

On the way to another tiny island, we saw some tourists jumping from the boat into the Mediterranean where the warm springs were spewing out of the caves at the base of this island.

"Hey, babe, are you wearing your suit? C'mon. Let's jump in."

"Gene, hold on. How do you know what's in the water?"

"Only one way to find out. Give your purse to the tour guide, take off your clothes, and hold my hand!"

Shrieking as we hit the water, I immediately felt the difference in temperature, surprisingly warm. In that moment, and so many other moments over the years, Gene and I left behind the constraints that we all must live with: the rules that adults live by; the work we do to live; the civility we learn to get along in the world. As we freely floated in that warm, Mediterranean water, we delighted in our surroundings, secure in our love for each other.

Gene's delicious sense of spontaneity has excited me on occasions like this for many years now. I'm always gratified when he's successful at breaking down my wall of fear and I just let go.

We splashed around a bit with the others, and I was glad Gene had put his other hearing aid in my purse. Thirasía, the tiny island where we docked on the way to Oìa on the mainland, had many steps to climb to get to a tavern on the way to the top. After huffing and puffing with many rest stops, all we wanted was a Coke. But I had lived in Greece and I knew all about Greek protocols; it would be rude to take up a table without ordering some food. We ordered an appetizer that we had no desire to eat, and left some cash on the table. When in Rome . . .

Our four days on this popular tourist island was a madcap rush, because there was so much to see. But our time there was well-spent. After flying back to Athens, we rested for a couple of days, and then we drove up to Kifisia to see my old friends, Eleni and her husband, Nondas.

Thomas Wolfe reminds me that I can't go home again: nothing is the same after nineteen years. Time doesn't stop. Everything changes. Trees grow taller. I couldn't find my old house on the street where I'd lived with Angel and our children. And then, I spotted it, nearly hidden amid all the Cyprus trees, like a nugget in a still stream. It's still there, though much of the stucco is crumbling at the corners. Like people.

But I'm glad I got to see it before it fell apart. It was a window into a time of great sadness and upheaval for me. I was recalling life with Angel and the children from thirty years earlier with a new and healthier perspective. Six months prior to this trip, I had given up alcohol and overuse of all substances. April 25, 2017, my sobriety date, was a milestone for me.

In 1987, I was desperately unhappy—with myself, with my mothering, and with my marriage. I'd undertaken little or no spiritual growth for most of my life—settling for a deep dissatisfaction that kept me mired in self-flagellation. I hadn't begun drinking much at that point, but I still went through periods of bulimia, gorging myself with volumes of high-calorie food, then secretly vomiting.

Three decades later, it was such a relief to go back there and be free of those compulsions. I was learning how to live life on life's terms, one day at a time, no longer hiding from the pain of it with food, or pills, or alcohol.

My friend had read in letters about the love of my life for more than two decades, and I daresay her mouth was watering just dying to meet him. Eleni's memories of me, still buxom and un-lined in early middle age, did not conform with who I had aged into. And her fantasies of Gene from many years before were likely superior to the man who stood in front of her.

Eleni, her face deeply lined from years of sun damage and smoking, was a beautiful example of European women and their unapologetic attitude about age. *Good for you Eleni, you can celebrate all that you are without the artifice of makeup or plastic surgery. I wish I had your self-confidence!*

Nineteen years is a long time. But feeling the warmth of her embrace and seeing her affirmation as our eyes locked onto each other, it was as if no time had passed.

That evening, after Gene had gone to bed, Eleni and I strolled into the plaza for a treat and sat down in an outdoor café.

"Two ice creams," my friend ordered. Then she turned to me. "*Ti thelis, mana mou?*"

"Vanilla, thanks," and then I added, "with chocolate syrup."

"I'll have strawberry," she told the server scribbling our orders, "but mine with whipped cream."

I waited to tell her in person about Annie, and when I did, my eyes tearing up, she shed no tears but said matter-of-factly as though she'd been in the recovery rooms for years, "Marilea, you cannot help her if she doesn't want help. Let her go. Concentrate on your other children and grandchildren."

"Yes, you're right, Eleni. I've spent fifteen years learning what you just told me in one minute."

"Bravo, Marilea," she concluded, taking my hand.

I could accept what she told me—without resistance.

The next day before we drove up to her beach house, I lit a candle for my daughter in the Greek Orthodox Church nearby and prayed that she'd find peace—in this life or the next.

And I let her go.

We left Athens after a couple of days and drove north to the city of Volos. Nondas' family comes from that area, and he and Eleni keep a second home there.

Volos may or may not be a captivating city, but it's Nondas' home, and that's all that matters. Greeks' roots burrow deep into the soil, and where they come from speaks to who they are. They wear their home proudly like a badge, with everything that goes with it: from different ways to dance the hasapiko to an almost feverish need to eat a lot of fish, regardless of the cost.

I've always envied that about Nondas: his fierce love of and appreciation for his roots—along with the kinship that often goes with it. I'd never enjoyed that secure sense of belonging.

Not until I moved to Camano Island with Gene. This was where my recovery journey peaked. I've learned to be at home with myself. And, maybe not coincidentally, I've found my long sought-after home as well.

Volos is the entryway to the Pelion Peninsula, which looks like an inverted boot on a map, sticking out into the Aegean Sea. Nondas and Eleni, as well as their daughter and her family, own houses right on the water on this jut of land.

Our hosts asked Gene and me how we wanted to spend our time there, and at first I tried to find a convenient ferry to Ski-athos, one of the islands in the Northern Sporades. But when I learned how inconvenient the price was—and remembering how many of the Greek Islands I'd already seen—we agreed that a car tour of the Pelion Peninsula was a better idea. We weren't disappointed.

There is only one main road along the spine of this boot-shaped landmass, but we whizzed along in our rented car as though it were a four-lane highway. Our destination was the island of Trikeri, a little stone kicked off the toe of the boot in the Pagasetic Gulf, part of the Aegean Sea. We underestimated the time it would take to arrive there, and, as we had on other trips, we were late getting started.

Many times in our travels, we've missed out on our final destination. This often happened because Gene had lost his focus. He got distracted; he was too busy enjoying the scenery along the way.

"Gene, c'mon! We'll never catch the ferry if we don't hurry up," I said, pressing him to get back in the car. He was unmoved.

"Babe, come over to this viewpoint. Have you ever seen such colors in rocks? What time is it? Three? The sun is illuminating these striations right now. But it won't last. In an hour, it'll look just like another rock. Come see it before it disappears."

Gene has helped ease me off the treadmill I've been on all of these years. Long before I met him, I'd been driven much of the time, always endeavoring to get from Point A to Point B, oblivious to what I could see along the way. How much I've missed, I don't know.

With Gene as my partner, it's as though I've gained another pair of eyes.

We never made it to Trikeri. As the sun was going down, we knew we had to turn around to make it back to Eleni's house safely. The roads were not well-made. They were curvy and slick, and there were no streetlights. So we continued back toward Volos, stopping at a seaside village for a slice of pizza.

"You never made it to Trikeri?" Eleni chided me upon our return. "That's the best part of a trip along the peninsula. How could you miss out on the point of the drive? I'm sorry you didn't get to see it," she moaned, shaking her head at our decision to turn back.

"Eleni, don't worry. We enjoyed the trip very much," I assured her. "Gene and I just wanted to see something before it disappeared."

Toward the end of my marriage, I had dared to dream that I could still find my own voice and make a difference in the world. Gene's loving presence on this trip to Greece was a constant reminder of the choice I'd made back in 1992. *"Marilea-mou, állaxes. Eínai ypérocho na vlépeis."* (Marilea, you have changed. It's lovely to see.)

Time. How it transforms us, and the world around us. Everything has changed, nothing is the same. Nearly thirty years ago, I'd prayed that the leap I was about to take with Gene would be worth it. I have never regretted my decision.

Christmas on the Big Island

Two months later, my whole family took the long, six-hour flight to Kona, Hawaii, this time to celebrate my seventieth birthday. This Pacific island was a place apart from any of the other islands I'd seen.

"How can we have Christmas without a tree, Bela? Everyone has colored lights, see?" Emily was pointing out some colored lights strung on the bushes in the park and in a few windows.

"You kids will figure it out. Be creative! Believe me, this is one Christmas you will want to remember."

Quinn and Emily made their own Christmas tree out of what was handy. They found a three-foot pole in the hall closet and we had just enough green construction paper to cut out some big, tropical-looking leaves.

"Construction paper leaves?" I asked, wrinkling my nose. "Let's go outside and find some real ones."

"Okay," piped in Emily. "I saw some big yellow ones near the rock back there," she said, pointing to a huge boulder on the golf course.

"Great. Let's go gather them before they blow away. Do we have scotch tape in the house?"

"Yes, but we may need to buy more," Quinn pointed out.

After a quick trip to the local market, Quinn and Emily finished making a tropical Christmas tree, a little lopsided, but perfect in its imperfection. On Christmas morning, the real focus would be all of the wrapped presents waiting to be opened.

Every day for a week, we played croquet on our back lawn, we swam in the two pools, we relished having dinner outside as we watched the red ball in the sky disappear below the horizon. One beach after another, not all of them good for snorkeling, but we found one and jumped off the rocks to observe the colorful fish. I had to wear a wetsuit, because the Pacific water felt chilly to this East Coast girl.

Kilauea Volcano is situated on the southeast part of the island, south of Hilo, and we all drove over there to explore the area. When I lived in Nicaragua in 1977, I fearlessly hiked up to the mouth of the Masaya Volcano and observed the red lava flowing far down below. I was carrying my infant son in a pouch, but I maintained a safe distance on the viewing platform. Now that son was standing beside me as we watched the fiery volcanic activity in Hawaii.

One thing that made this vacation out of the ordinary for me was my "now-family." My daughter Caroline from San Francisco, my son Carter and his family, Gene and I, all having a really good time together. With all of us living on the West Coast, it was eminently doable, and Carter made it happen.

The best gift this Christmas was being our best selves. Three things helped me to achieve that:

Just show up. *Resist the temptation to isolate and hide.*

Make an effort. *Try to put my best foot forward. Be mindful of what I say to others.*

Accept and love people where they are. *Don't try to manipulate or change anyone.*

The rest is magic.

My family showed up and made the effort to celebrate me. Carter wrote a poem for me and had it framed:

"She is like the sea:

A life of giving

To all who need."

Receiving those generous words from my grown son was a watershed moment for me. I realized then that I'd been a good-enough mother to my three children. I'd had serious doubts over the years. But I taught my children right from wrong, I gave them a safe place to grow up, I taught them the value of a dollar, I passed on the rewards of hard work, and I encouraged them in school. Most importantly, I loved them without condition and still do. All three of them.

Losing Annie to the cruelty of substance use disorder has led me on a journey of self-discovery that I never expected to make in my lifetime. Through my own recovery work, I've managed to let go of my daughter—and to survive losing her—by embracing a better life for myself.

Two months earlier, during Gene's and my trip to Greece, I'd found what I'd been looking for.

It was now easier to recall my eight- and ten-year-old little girls, playing on their balcony and sliding down the banister to the backyard.

"Mom," Annie had called out to me, "you've always loved the coral roses best. Take a picture of me and Oscar in front of this bush."

"Annie, hold him still. Does the dog need to be in every picture?"

"Yes, Mom. He's part of our family."

And now, thirty years later, I hold fast to those memories as I put them in a back drawer. I have turned out to be a happier mother than my mother, and I believe I'm giving my best self to my children and my grandchildren, to Gene, to my friends, and to myself.

How do I describe a broken glass in need of repair? What can I do?

I glue the pieces together.

"Oh no," my evil twin tries to upset me, *"you can see all the breaks! It's not seamless; it's not perfect."*

"Correct. It's who I am. Perfect in all my cobbled-together messiness. And on April 25, 2017, I stopped drinking alcohol and overusing all substances, one day at a time."

"Good luck with that," she smirks.

"I'm sober today, without any substances to dull the pain in my life," I tell her.

"Have a glass of wine instead! Maybe two or three. Then you won't feel anything!"

My evil twin is a seductive liar. I see the game now. I send her scurrying back to her corner, permanently sulking as I walk away.

With a new sense of freedom, I can relax and just be me. Imagine that! No more masks. No more drunken embarrassments. The gift of my sobriety spills over onto Gene, the rest of my family, and all my friends.

And their gift to me? They love me, anyway, in all my flawed humanity.

"You've taken me, and our wee small ones, to Hawaii's Kona Coast.
And you and I spent weeks seeing Greece—Santorini to Volos.
Marvelous remembrances
All.
But best of all has always been
Sharing such times with you,
My one and only love."

—Happy Birthday to Toots from Gene, 1/9/18

The Sound of Water

COVID-19 has taught us patience. During the pandemic, Gene and I mostly stayed home. Every few months, we took a short trip somewhere, a little rebellious and reckless. Yes, we were, but not like when we were younger. We still needed to remind ourselves that there was a world out there. Now, we are haltingly returning to our activities that used to sustain us and give us purpose.

Every day when we go down to our beach, we strain our eyes looking for a white sail out on the water. Gene still dreams of sitting at a tiller watching the sails fill with wind. That has been his long-deferred dream.

In the meantime, we have contented ourselves paddling up and down Saratoga Passage in our beloved Malecite. This forty-five-pound Kevlar canoe has been all over the country with us, from Quetico Provincial Park to Glacier National Park. We couldn't imagine our small fleet of boats without it.

Until November 2020, and the king tide that tore it apart.

Usually, we were careful to leave the canoe in its spot high away from the water at the loading dock. But on this last paddle, we left it on the beach, ready for an early paddle the next morning when the tide would be in. We put it up high, near the face of the cliff descending onto the beach. Surely, it would be safe there.

Waking up the next morning, we saw the sky and the wind telling us all we needed to know. Without even gulping down a cup of coffee, we raced down to the beach, got out of the truck, and stood in disbelief as we watched the king tide hammer the hull out of our Malecite.

No, not a play on words. The hydraulic power I had learned to respect from years of canoeing with Gene was fast tearing into the hull of our boat. And the rails that Gene had already twice replaced looked like loose pieces of kindling, torn up and mangled.

"God," I stammered, as though my words could make it stop.

I started to go down to it, like a mother rescuing a drowning child.

Gene grabbed me by the arm. "Stop!" he bellowed as the waves crashed menacingly against the rocks below us. "She's gone, babe. She's gone," he conceded.

Stunned from bearing eyewitness to the death of our favorite canoe, we couldn't stand to watch any more of it. After about ten minutes we turned away, got into the truck, and drove back home.

Not a word between us about what had just happened. For the rest of the day, we shuffled around the house, avoiding each other, looking up at the sky from time to time in a giant rebuke. *Really, God? You couldn't have waited one day to demonstrate the power of your malevolent king tide?*

Gene quietly went down to the beach the next afternoon after the tide had receded. Lifting the crippled canoe over his head, he slogged through the shallow water and mud around the jetty and up the ramp. He tied it to the roof of my car, drove it home, and retired it to a couple of sawhorses under the deck behind the Revelation, hidden from view. I couldn't bear to look at her.

It took me weeks before I brought up the subject.

I blamed Gene for recklessly leaving our Malecite on the beach. And he blamed me, if I knew so much better, for being too passive. I should have insisted on bringing it up to the dock. When tragedy happens, there is always someone to blame. But we kept our thoughts to ourselves and let them simmer.

Sometimes, simmering brings things to a boil. And sometimes, the fire just goes out.

We did address all of this several months later, but without the heat of passion. Yes, we made a mistake. And yes, we lost our boat as a result. She was another one of our losses.

How many times have we accepted what we could not change? How many times have we struggled to move on and not stay mired in sadness and loss?

Maybe this was a God moment of one door closing and another one opening.

Perhaps it was time to look for another boat.

The breeze out of the south
rumples the wavelets of the Passage
and the curve of the beach blends
the small surf sounds, soft, soothing,
with the shower's timpani on the
Ranger's roof.

A small squall lingers and hides
for the moment the low wooded ridge
that forms Whidbey Island perhaps
three miles across the water. The water
sparkles where the sun burns through,
just ahead.

—Gene, 2017

The Last Sail

Late summer, after Labor Day 2005. Lewes felt lonely,
but Marilea and I found a man with a catamaran
on the sand
as we walked the quiet shore,
    and I asked, after some small talk,
    if we could sail it and he said absolutely

and off we went.

As I recall,
when I beached that boat,
I hoped I'd return one day
with a better craft.

Sailing memories from Lewes
hold mainly Mobjacks and Sailfish
    and Sunfish and one big
    sloop, a Dickerson 32.

Lord how I miss it, all of it,
spray and chop and wind and calm
and morning sun and western skies as night comes on
    from the water
    under sail.

—Gene, February 2016

Closing the Circle

"And the world cannot be discovered by a journey of miles, no matter how long, but only by a spiritual journey, a journey of one inch, very arduous and humbling and joyful, by which we arrive at the ground at our own feet, and learn to be at home."
—Wendell Berry

May 2021 was a spring like no other that I can remember. My whole world began to feel brighter, vibrant and more alive as I noticed the soft sounds and minute textures and colors I had overlooked before. For the first time since we'd lived on the island, our purple irises bloomed in all their glory. My lilac bush, too, blossomed for the first time since we'd lived here, delightfully ambrosial. Everything around us seemed more beautiful. Was it true or just my perception of things? Coming out of the bleak winter of COVID-19, the whole world seemed brighter to me.

We had grown weary of owning two houses, ready and anxious to sell the property in New Mexico. We knew exactly where we wanted to spend the rest of our days. Our love of water provided the connective tissue early in our relationship, and it has culminated in our home on Camano Island.

It couldn't have been a better time to sell our house in New Mexico. People with a lot of cash to spend—money that had been sitting in the bank with no place to spend it during COVID-19, combined with low interest rates—set up favorable conditions for anyone selling property.

"Marilea," my agent gushed, giddy with delight. "You've got three offers on the house, the first one sight-unseen. Someone in Colorado just wants an investment here. The second buyer, I can tell you, really fell in love with all of your colorful paint and tile work. And the third offer is just under the second one. The second one might be your best bet. Think about which offer you want to accept."

"Okay, let's see what number two's agent has to say. In a seller's market, I shouldn't have to sacrifice too much. But I don't want to draw this out. I want my cash in the bank as soon as possible. Gene and I have plans." I smiled, thinking about boats and salt air.

We delighted in the brief bidding war for our house, and we settled on the good prospect suggested by my realtor as we bid the house farewell.

That state, though, is a stunning, even intoxicating, place. We knew we'd be back to visit.

September and October start to usher in autumn in Albuquerque, a gorgeous and productive lingering—well past Thanksgiving—with a long harvest season and the farmers' markets overflowing with abundance. The tree leaves change color from the frosty night air, a welcome change from the oppressive heat of summer. The cottonwoods, in particular, turn bright yellow, not the reds I was used to seeing at their peak in New England.

And in the Rio Grande River valley, steady rows of those saffron cottonwoods flow north to south, filling the eyes with wonder.

Still, Gene and I missed that part of both of our childhoods when we were sailing on the water. And now, with the sale of the New Mexico house, that dream was within reach. With a small portion of our cash settlement, Gene set about looking for another boat for going back and forth in Saratoga Passage. The other day, he showed me a picture of an inflatable catamaran in his *Sail* magazine.

What?

We'd have to blow it up first?

With our lungs?

We Grow Older . . .

"Babe, are you free to hop in the car and bring me my camera? The big lens too," Gene asked me over the telephone. He was excited.

"What for?"

"Rainier is gorgeous, today. I need to get some shots."

"Honey," I responded impatiently, "you've captured that image from the jetty many, many times."

"It's even better today. C'mon, bring me my camera, okay?" he insisted. "I want you to see this yourself."

There's no getting bored with Gene. He sees everything as though it were for the first time.

"Don't tell me the beach and Rainier look the same today," he chides me as I arrive with his camera. "It changes every day. Every single day. You're just not being observant."

"If you say so," I respond.

In all of our years together, Gene has tutored me in many things, but his greatest gift to me has been the gift of curiosity. He has given me a new sense of wonder at sights I used to take for granted, never tiring of the beauty around him and sharing it with me. Last week, he called me on his way home.

"Hey, babe, go out on the deck and take in the sunset right now! Just stop what you're doing and take a look. The colors are different, today."

"Thanks, honey," I told him from the deck. "You're right. It is prettier today, but the sun is dropping fast."

"It always does," he said as he hung up.

When Gene and I met, we were on the far side of young, and that's stretching it.

We had teenage kids, jobs, and responsibilities. But—as young people might—we pushed the envelope, over and over.

We'd both spent much of our young adulthood fulfilling expectations, others,' and sometimes our own. Neither of us would wish away for a second the years before we met. During those years, we watched our five children grow up. Our partners at the time gave us many happy and lasting memories.

But—young or old—after all the hills and mountains we'd tackled, I thought I had done enough uphill trekking.

I hadn't.

Rainier National Park is located about one hundred fifty miles from where we live on Camano Island, but we have paid no attention to this natural wonder. It might as well have been in South Carolina for all the homage we paid to it. How have I taken it for granted for so long?

Gene hasn't, not at all. There isn't a low tide at our beach when he doesn't walk out through the mud and all the clams' air bubbles to strain his eyes to see Rainier. It's only ninety miles away as the crow flies. Some days, he's successful, but most days, this fourteen-thousand-foot active volcano is shrouded in the very weather it creates. It's almost always wrapped in a cloud. On clear days, it's a marvel to look at.

The first time we were at Rainier it was not pleasant. In the summer of 2002, we had just finished hiking up Mount St. Helens, and we were thoroughly exhausted. Still, we were so close, so we drove into the park a few hours later in a pounding, drenching rain and set up our tent in one of the campgrounds. We passed our time inside the tent, waiting for the rain to stop.

It didn't. We lay on the floor of that tent for twenty-four hours, turning from side to side like chickens on a rotisserie spit, squishing bugs, sniping at each other, reading for relief, sleeping, but really just waiting for the sun to shine. Patience was not my strong suit then, and I voted to pack out and go to Glacier National Park in Montana. Gene wasn't big on patience either, and he agreed. So that's what we did, never dreaming that we'd be living in Washington State twenty years later.

Rainier was another stellar project of John Muir's. Gene's love of nature and all things outdoors naturally pointed him to these parks. Early on, this became one of Gene's missions: to show me my own country, since I'd already seen much of the world through Angel's career assignments. And—as Gene has joked many times over the years—I'm a cheap date. It takes very little to bowl me over. Pay the entry fee, provide me with a tent that stays dry inside and a good pair of hiking boots, and I'm all in.

In recent years, however, we've graduated from tents to crummy motels and even a yurt last year. Sometimes, we do splurge and rent a nice B&B.

Once in the Elwha rain forest on the Olympic Peninsula, it poured the whole time as we tried cooking in our tent alcove and generally felt miserable because we weren't there to be sitting in a soggy tent waiting for the sun to shine. So I have concluded that tent-camping was a fun part of our younger years, but now I need to be comfortable.

Gene disagrees with me. He would be very content living in one of his many tents. But he has deferred to me for the past several years. It would be no fun for him to weather my discomforts. Even when I was much younger, I wanted to be comfortable. Summer weather in the Southwest could be scorching outdoors; and I didn't want to get any big blisters that might hobble me.

Back in 2004, we took a ten-mile hike to Jackson Lake in Grand Teton National Park in Wyoming. It was completely flat, but my feet hurt so much that I traded my boots for tennis shoes and made Gene carry my boots.

A few years later, we were camping just outside of Arches National Park in Utah, a popular destination in Moab. We had to settle for a small site down near the Colorado riverbed amid the trees and the bugs. We were so hot—our clothes soaked through with sweat and dirt—that we tried to go swimming in the Colorado River to cool off. As we waded into the muddy mire on the bank, we both sank down to our thighs far too quickly and decided we weren't that hot. Wide-eyed and frightened, twisting around to face the safety of shore, we tried to lurch forward, but our legs continued sinking into the cool mud. Right on cue, I panicked and screamed, but Gene grabbed my hand and pulled me with him as we desperately tried to stay upright. Gratefully, we squished our way back to solid ground.

That would have been quite an undignified end to all of our adventures.

And Arches isn't a state park: it doesn't have free showers!

So, as we approached the majestic Paradise entryway to some of the easier, more accessible trails at Rainier, we sat on the benches watching the visitors. Such an amazing variety of people: there is the young couple, I'd say in their thirties, with dad carrying their baby boy, and mom with the selfie extender so they could get a shot of the three of them. They continued on up the stairs as they decided which hike to take. There was a large group of tourists from Japan, some of whom have come over annually to work on the grounds around Rainier.

Hiking on the Myrtle Falls trail, we met two couples from Gig Harbor who walked just ahead of us. The climb was getting difficult, and Gene and I had to stop frequently. We walked at a leisurely pace—not in any hurry—ex-smokers with unhealthy lungs. I guess those couples decided on another route, since they turned around and passed us going back.

Stopping at a familiar bush, I turned to Gene, "Honey, look, blueberries!"

"No, they're not. Too small. And a different leaf," he said, correcting me.

We had just eaten our lunch, thinking it would fortify us to go farther. It didn't. We went up a little more, but I'm pretty good at reading Gene after all our hiking together. I knew when he was out of steam. I could have pushed him farther. I could have been competitive. But we're still together after nearly thirty years because, among other reasons, I knew when to back off and settle for peaceful collaboration.

Besides, I was tired too. We're partners, not competitors.

"Let's go back, okay?" Gene said.

"Sure, that's good," I conceded.

So we agreed to end the upward climb toward the viewing point on that trail. "One of the easiest ways to get close to viewing the Nisqually Glacier," we had read in our trail guide. Yes, I felt a little disappointed. Twenty years earlier, we had hiked without difficulty to Grinnell Glacier in Glacier National Park.

But that was twenty years before. Our lungs hurt, and we decided to go back down. Now the knees and thighs would hurt. We had reached our limit that day, and we knew it. Watching a younger man jogging uphill as he passed us, we felt no sense of failure. We knew who we were.

Acceptance.

On the way back down. I saw a woman picking those blueberries, and I approached her.

"Are they blueberries?"

"Oh, better than blueberries. These are mountain blueberries, and even sweeter," she cooed, squashing them with her tongue.

Intrigued, I picked a couple and tasted them, excitedly agreeing, "Oh, delicious!"

Gene was with me, and said, "Well, I stand corrected." I like that about Gene: when he's wrong, he admits it.

It takes time to see much of the beauty of Rainier. But we only hiked there for three days. The first day was an easy hike, a warm-up. We observed a 150-foot evergreen rooted to its nurse log. The second day was the challenging hike among the blueberries, about two miles up and back down. And, as if to bless us on our way down, a lovely doe, the first of the fauna we had seen on our trek that day, squatted down in the meadow just above us and did her business while a few tourists howled in laughter and tried to snap just the right picture of her sitting on her haunches.

The last day we were too tired to do anything more than a few more easy hikes. I wobbled along those easy paths dreaming of being horizontal. Acceptance again.

It's a state of grace.

"So, babe, what was your favorite part of our hike?" Gene asked me as we left Rainier.

"Two favorite things. The first was noticing all the goodwill among the hikers. People couldn't have been more helpful to each other, suggesting a better path, warning us about a bad one. Just general goodwill. Coming out of the pandemic and all the divisions in our country now, it was gratifying to see people treating each other with so much kindness and humanity."

"The other thing I loved was the way you and I, when it comes to uphill hiking, are on the same page. I told you many years ago that I had nothing to prove, that I was done with mountain hiking. And yet, we persisted, with me probably whimpering behind you wishing I'd been more assertive. But here we are, absolutely enthralled with the (melting) glaciers and blooming meadows of Rainier. I know we'll be back."

Carter hiking with his kids.

On the way home, we stopped in Seattle for a pizza and salad dinner with my son and his family. He had recently returned from an overnight backpacking expedition in the Pinchot National Forest. Carter was barely able to contain his excitement at his first trek into the wilderness with a hiking buddy. He proudly showed us all of his pictures of the beautiful natural landscape, along with his pictures of the night sky and the Big Dipper. He couldn't wait to repeat the experience, the next time with his wife.

Gene and I drove home, tired but deeply gratified by the beauty we saw and by seeing my son doing much of what we did twenty-five years earlier.

We've started to pass the mantle on to him and his family.

Aging With(out) Dignity

Fall 2021 passed uneventfully. Christmas was quiet, and two weeks later, the kids came up from Seattle again to celebrate Marilea's 74th birthday.

Then, toward the end of January, we were roused from our complacency.

I had been sleeping pretty soundly when Marilea let out a piercing yelp that got me up quick. I woke up enough to realize she was in the bathroom, so I walked across our small bedroom in the dark and turned on the bathroom light. Marilea lay moaning on the floor, parallel to the foot-tall tile wall lining the bathtub. She had apparently slipped on a towel and fallen.

My brain was not functioning at full capacity. "What happened?" She moaned a vague, unintelligible response. "Did you hit your head?"

"No," she whispered.

"Can you move?" I tried to look at her eyes, but her position on the floor made that impossible. She squirmed a bit, wiggled a bit, and I said, "Let me help." Slowly, I helped her get to her feet.

"Did you come in here to pee?"

"Yes."

"Did you pee?"

"Not yet." I helped her walk the few steps to the toilet.

She peed, and we slowly returned to the bed. I turned on a heating pad and gave her four Advil. Then I went downstairs for some cold packs.

I thought she may have cracked a rib when she fell. There was no visible bruising or swelling, so I was thrown off. I didn't realize how badly she had hurt herself.

My medical training was negligible—some school-related first aid, a little wilderness training, and CPR certification. None of that came into play. She said she hadn't hit her head. I thought the best thing to do was to get her into bed.

That night was most uncomfortable. She fell off to a fitful sleep, but I had trouble getting any rest. After an uncomfortable day and night, she appeared no better, but still showed no swelling or discoloration. I took her, anyway, to the Skagit urgent care facility an hour away.

From there, she was ambulanced to the closest facility with a CT machine, a hospital in Sedro-Woolley. The results showed six rib fractures, four of them displaced, a C-6 cervical fracture, and a collapsed lung (a pneumothorax). Because of the lung injury, she had to have a chest tube surgically inserted to drain out some accumulated air and blood. She woke up on another ambulance ride, speeding down to Seattle where there was an available bed at Harborview Hospital. Since that hospital is ninety miles from our home on Camano Island, and no visitors were allowed at hospitals anyway, I went home.

Because hospitals were overwhelmed during the pandemic—leading to shortages in personnel and equipment—I spent my first night in a bed in the emergency room. I was lucky that there was a bed at all for me in any hospital.

Except for having my babies, that was my first overnight stay in a hospital. My neighbor in the ER was a methamphetamine user seeking relief from multiple infected sores on her arms. Drifting in and out of consciousness the short time I was there, I asked the nurse what she was injecting into my vein.

"Dilaudid."

A few hours later, she was giving me more of something.

"Now what are you giving me?"

"Fentanyl."

The following morning, they spirited me up to the pediatric intensive care unit on the ninth floor. The hospital needed to free up the ER, and the pediatric ICU had the only other available bed. In my unit, individual spaces were separated by curtains. My neighbor up there was a heroin user. He was being given massive blood transfusions to keep him alive after an internal injury. The next day, they moved me to a regular room down on the seventh floor. My roommate was a fentanyl user, groaning in agony from surgery the day before. Begging for more pain relief, the doctors were mainlining as much methadone into her as they dared.

What were the odds of my three roommates being substance users? In today's world in the United States, apparently, they were substantial.

Still, Harborview Hospital felt like a palace to me. I enjoyed the view of Seattle from my window on the ninth floor, though I wondered where I'd be in an earthquake. I was in for a treat, with around-the-clock care from a flotilla of nurses. I made friends with my Vietnamese nurse in the ICU, who really warmed up to me when I told him I used to teach newly arrived immigrants like him.

"Why did you become a nurse?" I asked Binh.

"I knew early on that I wanted to be a nurse. I'd seen in Vietnam what a difference they make to help sick people, especially in the countryside. My parents and I ended up in Alabama when we arrived here. A good education was the most important thing to them. So they helped me as much as possible to get through school."

"How fortunate that you had such wise parents. How was it when you first got to the United States?"

"It was really rough learning the new language. But we had special teachers, like you were, who knew how to teach us English quickly. I'll always be grateful to them."

When I left that floor, he gave me a rose.

Binh's gesture pleased me beyond words.

I thought of my daughter Annie as I napped on and off during my four days in the hospital. While I was enjoying first-rate care, I also saw firsthand the sheer magnitude of the substance use catastrophe that is burdening our country. It's not a new problem, but the COVID-19 pandemic and other social grievances have only exacerbated it. We are a nation in deep, psychic pain, now more than ever.

I remember my three roommates as I move on with my life in recovery, both physical and spiritual. I wonder about Annie's last two decades, how many times my daughter has been one of those tortured souls. There was one time, a dozen years ago, when doctors in Virginia fought to save her femoral artery. How many other times has she been hospitalized since then? I just don't know.

It'll never happen to me, I had assured myself, after viewing "I've fallen and I can't get up" ads on television. *Poor old ladies,* I used to think. My days of gloating are behind me now as I face my own mortality—and that of other old ladies—with far more kinship and compassion.

While I was in the hospital, my bodily functions were carefully scrutinized, inside and out. When the nurses clapped and congratulated me every time I loudly passed gas, I knew I wasn't young anymore. When Miralax became my new best friend, I knew I'd reached a new normal.

"You go, girl!" said my nurse, Rodi, encouraging me to keep the flatulence coming.

"Why is it good to pass gas, Rodi?" I inquired, as if I didn't know. I wanted to hear her explanation, anyway.

"My dear," she explained in a grandmotherly way, "don't be embarrassed. It's a sign that your intestines are still working normally. And that there are no blockages. The poop that needs to come out won't be far behind," she said with a wink.

"Oh, what a relief."

Now when my grandchildren can't contain their laughter after I pass gas, I tell them I welcome the farts as a sign of healthy digestion.

Pride. Self-sufficiency. Overconfidence. Those feelings were punctured like the rib that nearly pierced my lung during that fall. And once again, not for the first time, Gene provided me with constant help and encouragement. From chauffeuring me to endless doctors' appointments to waiting on me constantly at home. "In sickness and in health . . ."

I had become Gene's enthusiastic partner in a few outdoor sports. We took big risks white-water paddling down swollen rivers in Canada. We climbed mountains and hiked in wildernesses better-suited, perhaps, to younger adventure-seekers. We had a cross-country skiing getaway planned two days after my fall. Now I want to take up snowshoeing. And he's very content to go along. *Peaceful collaboration* . . . This is how we love each other as we are visibly aging: bending and swaying, flexible but strong.

This is such a good thing: to face my limitations without embarrassment or shame. My son and grandchildren saw the hideous wound on the left side of my chest where the chest tube had been, and they learned that Bela is not invincible.

Now they cherish and care for me ever more deeply, just as I am learning to cherish and care for myself more deliberately than before. Attitude is everything in life, and I'm happy to remain a teachable student.

Before I left the hospital, I gave my rose to Sandy, my last roommate. I would wish someone to extend the same kindness to Annie, wherever she is.

Spiritual recovery encourages me to keep my nose down, remain humble and grateful in all things. Oh, I can take pride in my accomplishments; I just don't stay there. I always go back to remembering how unimportant I am in the grand scheme of things.

Fretting about an invitation to speak at a recovery meeting, I asked Gene for advice:

"Honey, what will I say? I haven't spoken at a Speaker's Meeting in three years!"

"Babe, relax. Just speak from your heart. What you say isn't as important as the service you're offering by standing up there, sharing what you've learned and showing how your life is happier now. It's the message, not the messenger, that matters."

But when my surgeon said, "Nose in the air! Up! Up! Let that neck brace do its work!" I complied.

"Whatever you say, Doc. Far be it from me to question you. I know I've dodged a major bullet, and I don't want to blow it."

All my high heels were the first to go . . .

Time for handrails . . . night lights . . .

Sailing at Sunset

Sailing in Maui.

"Marilea," my friend had gushed beforehand, "We found the most spectacular white sand beach. Miles of it. And make sure to get up early enough for a sunrise meeting. It's worth the effort, trust me."

On our bucket list was a trip back to Hawaii and a visit to the island of Maui. A month after my fall, the guardian angel that has always been sitting on my shoulder once again worked her magic, and my surgeons cleared me to get on the airplane.

Many of our friends had raved about this island, so we were anxious to see it for ourselves. We had made plans several months earlier to go with my son and his family during February vacation, and the six of us hunkered down for the long flight over the Pacific.

I knew how much Gene longed to be in a sailboat, and there were several opportunities on Maui to go sailing, so I arranged for us all to go out together.

In Maui, we got what we paid for. I wanted to avoid a huge crowd, so we took a smaller boat with fewer people. Snacks and drinks were part of the excursion. A colorful sunset sail near Lahaina on the northwest coast was a balm for Gene and me, the two of us longing to go back to our childhoods for a little while. We reveled in the steady breeze the gods had graced us with that day. Few things are more disappointing than trying to sail on a windless day.

My uncle had a beautiful boat, the *Allegra,* that he kept moored at the Corinthian Yacht Club in Marblehead, MA. He and my aunt took Gene and me for a sail more than once while we were still living on the East Coast. His boat was a forty-five feet sloop, the same length as our chartered boat. On this sunset sail, Gene spent much of the time talking to the skipper, refreshing his memory about large sailboats and how to rig them.

We were there to watch the sails fill up, feel the hull of the boat glide along the water beneath us, and catch our breath as the vessel heeled suddenly in a gust of wind and then righted itself. In two hours, we tacked about five times, and watched a flotilla of humpback whales and a bunch of dolphins or "fake killer whales." And, the heavenly sunset.

My Seattle family is in the planning stages of living their best lives in Puget Sound. And, for us, that would include boats—all the joy and fun and versatility that they provide. Gene and I grew up on boats. Together and apart, we sailed on lakes, in harbors, and on the open sea. We paddled down bulging rivers, then daw-dled on lakes that looked like glass.

That little sailing junket in Maui provided a window for my family to imagine what sailing on a smaller scale could be like. My son, who had never enjoyed the thrill of boating when he was young, has recently taken an interest in sailing and went for a few lessons with his wife in Lake Washington near his home. Both grandchildren spent a week at sailing camp the previous summer. They loved it.

Gene and I are actively looking for a boat to replace the Malecite we lost. Maybe a small sailboat, or a kayak, or another canoe. Carter and his family enjoy coming to Camano Island. With another boat here—and two able teacher/grandparents—Saratoga Passage could become another classroom for Gene and me.

If we're very lucky, those of us in the over-seventy crowd get a few do-overs in life. But not without a certain amount of self-awareness, discipline, and a large amount of goodwill. Gene and I have been actively reinventing ourselves for quite a few years now. For many people, retirement is a death sentence. So I took up writing a decade ago, and I hope to get back to a little teaching. Gene continues to actively pursue his many interests, other than boats: music, gardening, and writing. Having so many common interests keeps us always connected, but we still do some things separately: Gene jams in two different musical groups, usually with his guitar or mandolin; I sing in a local chapter of the Threshold Choir, a compassionate group of women who gather to sing to people at the end-stage of life.

Gene and I continue to grow stronger in our "separateness," and our growth enhances the "us" that we have become. That we are still becoming.

As I write this, we are in active recovery from alcoholism—one day at a time. Gene has thirty-six years of sobriety. I recently celebrated five as I told a grateful Carter months ago.

When I was younger, I spent too many years straining to see the stars under the light of a full and radiant moon. *Youth really is wasted on the young,* I tell myself, determined to live every day with gratitude for the miracles promised in the rooms of recovery. I am humbled daily as I confront my defects, praying to be "relieved of the bondage of self." Slowly, with the help of Gene, my immediate family, and my recovery family, I can clearly see the light at the end of a long tunnel.

"Be the light," I tell my grandchildren. "Be the light for others."

"How Do I Love Thee . . . ?"

At our beach on Camano Island.

The lessons I've learned in life have brought me closer to an understanding of the mysteries of love. To me, love has everything to do with one of the Greek words for it: agápe. The Greeks certainly understood the difference between different kinds of love—eros being sexual love, for example—but agápe is the word for humanity's love for one another. My understanding of the word further leads me to an English word derived from it: agape, or open-mouthed.

Loving between two people almost always involves an openness of mind and heart. Gene and I had been hoping—this second time around—to embrace some of the lessons from our past for a greater purpose. We'd hoped to find a way to be happy together while still honoring our differences, even our whims at times.

We haven't always agreed on things, but we've either found a way around disagreements or laid them aside to look at later, without losing our individual integrity. These disagreements were costly at times. But we learned to look at these problems with cooler heads, figured out who was responsible for what, and tried to resolve them favorably. That's the most any couple can do when conflict arises. And because we loved each other, we were determined to work things through amicably—always hoping for the win-win.

Loving can be expansive. It has the capacity to make us bigger than we were before. I was thoroughly against gardening with Gene, much less running an orchard. But over time, seeing all the blood, sweat, and tears he put into his garden, and with such rich fruits of his labor, I began to feel swayed. By the time we moved to Camano Island, I'd opened my mind enough to work our backyard garden with him. And I've learned to love it. Loving Gene transformed me into a novice but enthusiastic gardener.

Gene has showed that same openness toward me and my needs. When we moved to Camano Island, putting us near my son and his family, Gene left part of his family behind in New Mexico. Bridget still lives there and is happy with her life in community theater. That was no small sacrifice for Gene. But we do spend money and time to go back and visit, reconnecting with Bridget, just as we do with Patrick in Virginia and Caroline in San Francisco.

"And the learning process must be coordinated so that
the actor learns as the other actors are learning and develops
his character as they are developing theirs. For the smallest
social unit is not the single person but two people.
In life too we develop one another."
—Bertolt Brecht

When I met Gene, I was at a point in my life where I craved independence. And Gene also enjoyed the freedom I encouraged him to explore. This was where we were when we met, and we found the ability to remain open to the challenges we faced. Rather than running from them, we let them shape us.

We worked hard to meet each other where we were—in our work lives, in our wilderness adventures, in our living arrangements, and in supporting our families. We learned early on that those families—whom we loved without exception—would have the ability to test us. We have walked with them through their trials—they, in turn, have helped Gene and me through ours. We can look at each other now with the certainty that we did our best for our children. And that—sincerely loving that part of each other that is separate—brought us closer together as a couple.

Gene and I developed each other's capacity to love well. We did our best to feed each other's good wolf. I blossomed, in midlife, by uniting with a man who loves me the way I am, and I him. And from that foundation we both grew in our willingness to try new things, secure in our faith about the mystery of love.

We can keep it if we don't hold on too tight.

Making Room

Pictures don't lie. They speak to us. They tell a story, a whole string of stories, to the observant eye.

We now live in a digital world where technology has revolutionized the taking of pictures and their preservation. Gene and I have been caught between two worlds of image-recording. And I'm still wedded to the old ways, proudly organizing the nine or ten albums of my life in pictures. Our adventures in the wild have been so numerous that one of the largest albums is devoted to just that trip one summer: the Argo fire in Quetico Provincial Park, the loon dance and everything that it symbolized. The start of our abiding love affair.

When I see my albums chronologically lined up on the bottom shelf of my bookcase, I see my life, and that of my children, represented in pictures. And, of course, there is a multitude of significant events not pictured in the albums. But I see much of my story, and that triggers memories of more.

I observe Gene now, the man playing his guitar on the deck by himself, serenading the birds, his face chiseled and deeply lined from years of smoking and sun exposure. The blonde, curly hair gone gray-and-white. But the same fit body I fell in love with twenty-nine years ago. The long legs muscled and firm from riding a bicycle when it was easier to get around Washington, D.C., that way.

"You always see more on a bike, Marilea," he pointed out, as I feared being hit by a car.

My father injured his thumbnail with a soldering iron while tinkering with his radios in our basement in the 1950s. Gene too worked in the trades for a few years before he got into teaching. He complains about being ham-handed, unable any longer to make his hands work for him. Our hands tell a story about us too.

When I visited my father's mother in the nursing home before she died, it was her hands I would never forget: crooked and bent, twisted and useless, the arthritic hands of a near-centenarian. And I am her granddaughter: not yet crippled, but some days I can't even open a jar. Like alcoholism, arthritis is a progressive disease that can be managed but not cured.

These are our inheritances: the snapshots and the stories they tell; the story behind the stories; the books and stories we publish as part of our legacies; the physical characteristics passed on to us even as we bequeath the same things to our children and grandchildren.

There is no end to our love story. But Gene and I have felt a contentment from writing it not just within the stories themselves, but in the way these experiences have changed us, nearly broken us, and yet, sustained us.

We felt like teenagers when we began our love affair, but we weren't. Maybe just anxiously trying to catch up. I was forty-five and wishing I'd spent more time in the outdoors when I was raising my children. Gene had longed to do more outdoor exploring himself.

I was an anxious and willing student. Gene showing up literally in my classroom took me right out of the instructor's seat and he became my teacher instead. He will never credit himself with the length and breadth of the lessons he has passed on to me. But my health and durability have everything to do with Gene's steadfastness, intelligence, and ability to manage my vulnerable nature.

Love has many different faces, but it endures.

Salt in the Wound

If what we've learned could spread to those around us . . .

We'll plant our love in the ground,
Like we would plant a tree,
And watch it grow as the years go by.

There will be a new generation growing in time.
Maybe they will want to watch the tree grow.

No salt in their wounds,
No memories to crush like an acorn
Into the earth.

We'll take them in our boats
And show them the splendor of nature
And teach them where contentment lies.

Not in the pain that preceded them,
But in the expectant joys that stretch before them.

You and I, old man, have survived to smell
The bitterness of the crushed acorn seed
Flowering into a new young tree.

—To Gene, with love from Toots, late spring 2017

Afterword

How did I get so lucky, to have found the water, the woods, the mountains, and all the outdoors—my sanctuary—in one simple man?

Such a hard-won attitude—the healing balm for my many wounds—is resonant of many longings and much desire to live happily ever after. This is a story about the power of love to offer resilience and necessary tools for molding, even transforming, the most vulnerable human beings. Gene's and my stories—a few hilarious, some of them sad—reflect the human condition in us all.

The future is always uncertain. An asteroid might hit our planet. Maybe we'll slaughter all the cows, become vegetarians, and breathe cleaner air. A tsunami could wash over our island in Puget Sound and turn us into boat people.

Not to worry. Tomorrow is just an idea. All will be well.

We still have today.

End Notes

Alcott, Louisa May, quoted in *Courage to Change* (New York: Recovery Family Group Headquarters, Inc., 1992).

Barber, Margaret Fairless, quoted in Karen Casey, *Each Day a New Beginning* (Center City, MN: Hazelden Foundation, 1982).

Berry, Wendell, *The Unforeseen Wilderness: Kentucky's Red River Gorge* (Berkeley, CA: Counterpoint, 2006).

Brecht, Bertolt, Ed. and Trans. John Willett, *Brecht on Theatre: The Development of an Aesthetic* (New York: Hill and Wang, 13th Edition, 1992).

Legrand, Louis, *The Tale of Two Wolves* (CreateSpace Independent Publishing Platform, 2017).

Lewis, C.S, *The Lion, The Witch, and the Wardrobe: A Story for Children* (New York: Harper, 2008).

Lindbergh, Ann Morrow., quoted in Karen Casey, *Each Day A New Beginning* (Center City, MN: Hazelden Foundation, 1982).

Nouwen, Henri, *With Open Hands* (Notre Dame, IN: Ave Maria Press, 2006).

Watkins, James N., Inspirational Quote Notebook (Independently Published, 2019).

Wolff, Tobias, *In Pharoah's Army: Memories of the Last War* (New York: Vintage, 1995).

Zaki, Zaki, *I Don't Need Therapy, I Just Need My Boat: A Boat Logbook For Those Who Love Boating and Track Your Adventure on the Boat* (Independently Published, 2022).

Acknowledgments

The stories detailed in this memoir are all true and capture the essence of two lives, well-lived. A few names and landmarks have been changed to guard the privacy of those involved. But the stories themselves are true to the best of Gene's and my recollection.

I want to thank Sheila Bender, founder of Writing it Real, and all the readers who have helped me develop and nurture my writing. I can't imagine publishing without the firm and objective touch of a skilled editor. Sheila encouraged me to fearlessly explore the fullness of my heart and commit it to the page.

The person I am today is the result of embracing the enlightenment and fellowship found in the twelve steps of recovery. A simple list of guidelines, but not easy to practice, the steps are a set of principles which, when followed, help me be the best person I can be.

And that—becoming a woman finally at home with herself—has been worth the long journey.

Thank you to our children: Carter, Annie, Caroline, Patrick, and Bridget. Thank you to our grandchildren: Quinn and Emily. A special thank you to their talented mother, Carrie, who worked magic on the pictures that illuminate so much of our story. Thank you, recovery family, every one of you, for my ongoing recovery.

Gene has been my touchstone for nearly thirty years. We have grown and matured in love and partnership with each other. My life is infinitely richer now, and for that, my love, I thank you.

About the Authors

Photo credit: Christopher Tuohy

Marilea's early life involved interfacing with several world cultures. In high school, she went to France one summer to study French. That whet her appetite for travel, and she volunteered as an English teacher on a mission in Puerto Rico for two summers. Her first husband joined the Foreign Service and for fifteen years they traveled from Nicaragua to Ecuador to Greece to Italy—with three children and a dog.

After her divorce, she moved on to the next phase of her life where she consolidated her cultural experiences with her vocation in the classroom. She was an English as a Second Language high school teacher for seventeen years in Virginia. She met her present partner, Gene, at this time. Toward the end of her teaching career, she earned a Master of Arts in teaching. That journey, a master's in reflective practice, was a critical tool toward understanding her own life journey.

Now in her third act, and retired from teaching, she has time to reflect back on her fortunate life, continue to learn and grow, and put some stories down on paper. Her two award-winning memoirs chronicled the generational substance use disorder in both herself and her daughter. Her third memoir, *Gene and Toots*, is a love story written with her partner about her ultimate recovery from the disease. We follow the couple traveling around the national parks in the United States, Canada, Greece, and Hawaii over the course of nearly thirty years. It completes this series of memoirs on substance use disorder.

Writing is an illuminating form of self-discovery, and it helps Marilea put her life into better perspective. This has proven to be valuable rite of passage for many men and women in their golden years, and she hopes to teach life-writing to seniors.

Gene Dunne grew up outside of Washington, D.C. He was married for a number of years and has two grown children. He taught high school English alongside Marilea for a dozen years before they decided to relocate to New Mexico. They bought a small house with two acres of land which Gene turned into a thriving orchard for nearly ten years. Then drought in the Southwest combined with growing family in Seattle convinced him to move with Marilea to an island in Puget Sound where they continue to garden. This final push westward enabled him to take his boats out of the garage and put them in the water around Camano Island. He spends his time playing music and jamming with friends. Marilea and Gene are thrilled to have ended up in the Pacific Northwest where they enjoy grandchildren, hiking, cross-country skiing, ice-skating, and walking on the beach.

Printed in the USA
CPSIA information can be obtained
at www.ICGtesting.com
JSHW011629061023
49651JS00008B/22

9 781958 808139